Traveling WITH JERICHO

A COOKBOOK MEMOIR

BY CHEF JERICHO MICHEL

First Edition

ISBN: 978-1-7361714-8-6 (hard cover)
          978-1-954614-01-7 (soft cover)

Michel. Jericho.
Traveling with Jericho.

Edited by: Amy Ashby, Lacey Cope

Cover Illustated by: Alexandra Bye

Published by Warren Publishing
Charlotte, NC
www.warrenpublishing.net
Printed in the United States

"You learn a lot about someone when you share a meal together."
–Anthony Bourdain

I dedicate this book to my family
... even the ones who don't like me.

ACKNOWLEDGMENTS

First, and for everything, I want to acknowledge my wife Mackenzie. She has guided me through some tough times and helped pave an open road for my life and for this book to come to fruition. My love, mi corazón. Okay ... mushy part out of the way!

To my daughter, for always being herself. She is the only human who can truly read my emotions and understand how to deal with them at all times, and she has become my greatest teacher.

To my father, for teaching me to believe in myself and helping me to find the confidence to discover who I am and what I believe in.

To my grandfather Joe, who passed away before I reached adulthood: ever since I was a small child, he inspired me to be a chef, and I always think of him during my proudest culinary moments.

To all of my Michel and Powers family, for being a part of this book—whether they knew it or not—and for helping to put some of the missing puzzle pieces together. Special thanks to Aunt Sue and Aunt Joanne for contributing some of their recipes, stories, and guidance.

To Rosie, for being a teacher and truly pushing me to get this book together and give it to the world.

To my Chicago Hearty Boys, Dan and Steve, for taking me under their wings as a young chef and showing me how to throw a great event anywhere.

To my Chattanooga guys, Ryan and Matt, for teaching me how to run a kitchen like a business and giving me a platform to grow and spread my wings in all aspects of this crazy industry a lot of us call home.

To Carter Lave, for being my sous chef in life—and I mean for real!

To Jon Carl, just for being Jon Carl! And for showing me that we can have fun doing this thing.

To Joan at The Laughing Seed, for creating a space where I can cook and continue to grow, even when I think I've got it all figured out.

To Parker, for pushing me to do what I try to pretend I don't want to do anymore.

To Randy and Jessamine Stone at Green Sage, for believing and letting us take over for a couple days to take the awesome photos for this book.

To Mindy and everyone at Warren Publishing, for contributing their hard work, dealing with my grammatical errors, and showing me a whole new passion I never knew I had.

To all the chefs, cooks, servers, bartenders, and people I've cooked for or with over the last twenty-something years: this book exists because of all the awesome memories you helped to create.

Last but never least in my eyes: to Anthony Bourdain, for showing me that I am a part of something special and for inspiring me to write about my adventures. I can only hope and dream that this book provides one single chef with the same inspiration that his books and career did for me.

Now this is where I drop the mic!

Thank you, and I love all of you!

The Terminal BrewHouse has partnered with The Trust for Public Land to add a little flavor to the fight to save Stringer's Ridge from overdevelopment.

'Old Baldy ESB' is back. This classic session beer is designed to refresh and stimulate both your taste buds and your desire to preserve the beauty and natural uses of Stringer's Ridge. We have not only vowed to give you a well rounded beer but to give some jack to the people that are dedicated to preserving the hiking and biking access to one of the most beautiful and approachable ridgelines in our fair city.

20% of the sales of Old Baldy will be donated to the cause for the month of September. While we can't endorse drinking to excess, we do encourage you to come in and drink ESB often, take home a growler, and carb up on this great beer for a great cause.

CONSOLIDATED FOODS CORP

L. H. PARKE

| SIZE | BRAND | | TOT |

ONE TRIBE FRIDAY JANUARY 21 2000
VIVID AND N20 A SPECIAL 2HR TAG
LEGACY   MEDICAL GRADE
XIST   KRE
ASHEVILLE   U.T.T.A. G
RHYMES   SCOTT B
LIFE   RYTHEM REBALS
till 6am
dio@hairspray   18+21 to drink
d st. asheville nc info 828-258-2027

400

The CITY TAVERN
2nd & Walnut St's
fine food & drink

...n the cooking of Germany

To Go MENU

one tribe fri. december 17 1999   7$
Rick Sierra, aka roll-x-satellite rec.
Sursee-Asheville
Instinct-starseed, DCM   for the people
Don 7-disco warriors   by the people
Scott-B-Asheville
18+21 to drink   doors will open at 11pm
ion-the basement of havana 113 broadway
828-250-0420   downtown asheville
8-670-6196   happy birthday aubury, and all the sag's

VI Traveling with Jericho

INTRODUCTION

This book is compiled of things I've learned, people I've met, places I've visited and lived, and all things related to my ongoing journey with—and passion for—food and travel. Over the years, I have worked to develop recipes for other chefs' cookbooks, always with the thought of writing my own one day. Finally, after years of prodding, my chef friends convinced me to do it. I have to thank my friend Rosie in particular; she inspired me to make my dream a reality.

◆◆◆

I was born into the business, as they say, being that my great-grandmother owned—and actually lived above—our family restaurant in Maple Shade, New Jersey. Most of the memories I have of her and my grandfather Joseph are based around food and growing up in and around the kitchens at Grandma Michel's house in Cinnaminson, New Jersey; the Michel Restaurant in Maple Shade; and at cookouts with my father's side, the Powers family.

My first job in a kitchen was when I was around fourteen years old and living in a rural western North Carolina town. I washed dishes and took out the trash. Nothing glamorous, but that's where it all started. I do remember spending maybe a day or two with my uncle Joe, who was working in an Italian restaurant in Highlands. I moved back to New Jersey soon thereafter, but believe me, I wasn't done cooking in North Carolina.

I have been cooking seriously for around twenty-three years now. I have cooked all up and down the east coast as well as running kitchens in Atlanta, Philly, Chicago, and southern Florida. I have opened, helped open, or re-opened four restaurants along with rebuilding quite a few kitchens. It was in Chicago that I discovered my passion for being a chef, but I learned how to really cook in Asheville, North Carolina where I now once again reside.

I am a true believer in good, honest food. I do my part in teaching others how to eat healthy, sustainable, local, and organic food. I eat this way as well (most of the time). I have developed a passion for learning new food and techniques, while still trying to make a living.

This book is a collection of memories, recipes, and techniques I have picked up, self-taught, and created with people who made an impact on my love of food. I've tried to pick recipes and fun stories that align with the different places I've lived, cooked, drank, and DJ'ed (my second passion!). I've also included my favorite drinks with each chapter, as well as songs to pair with each recipe—just for fun.

So, here it is: a cookbook for my friends, my family, and anyone and everyone who is as in love with food as I am.

Enjoy!

JERICHO'S KITCHEN BASICS

I want to provide you, my readers, with some tips I find helpful when running a home kitchen. These tactics trickle down from my time spent in professional kitchens—and they work! So I stick to them even when I'm at home.

There is (almost) always a solution to any problem in the kitchen. This is something I had to learn in order to survive in any kitchen, whether it be at home or at work. Nine times out of ten, you'll be able to fix a mistake! For example, if something is too salty, too sweet, over-cooked, under-cooked, or so forth, just take a deep breath and call on the great and powerful internet! Yes, I'm serious. I can't personally answer all of your questions—I'm still cooking for a living—but with just a little research, you can (almost) always find solutions to your culinary mishaps.

STOCK YOUR PANTRY

Keep the basics around because you never know when you'll want to get creative or impress your significant other or your friends. Here are the essentials:

OIL. Keep a couple of good ones around, maybe avocado oil for cooking and a good, dark virgin olive oil for finishing dishes with. (Note that darker-colored olive oils are richer and typically of a higher quality.)

FLOUR. Keep both fresh flour and gluten-free flour around. Even if you don't eat gluten-free, this may come in handy when entertaining for guests who do.

SPICES. Flaked kosher salt is a must, and then grab some fun spices. Some of my favorites are smoked paprika, turmeric, and oregano, which are very universal.

BEANS. Dry beans and legumes hold up well and taste great.

PASTA AND RICE. Some good pastas and rice. My personal favorites are linguine, penne, and farfalle for pasta; and basmati and arborio for rice.

STOCK. I love using leftover bones or veggies from dinner to make fresh stock to store in the freezer.

MULTIPURPOSE YOUR POTS AND PANS

Reusing pots and pans during meal prep is vital for your sanity—especially around the holidays. Try to utilize just one or two pots or pans when cooking a meal at home. Take a few minutes to plan it out ahead of time. For example: the water pot becomes the sauce pot, or the roasting pan becomes the veggie sauté pan.

CAST-IRON PANS ARE GREAT!

They last forever if cared for properly, they come in all shapes and sizes, and they hold up better than most sauteé pans. Plus, you can get your daily essential iron when you cook with them.

THE RIGHT BAKING SHEET

Get some larger, commercial-size baking sheets or "half-sheet" pans. While standard home baking sheets "quarter-sheet pans" are typically 9" x 13", half-sheets are 18" x 13", giving you a lot more real estate to work with. Once you use a real one, you'll never buy the silly at-home pans again. You can find them online. (Note, however, that "full-sheet" commercial pans will likely not fit in your home oven, so you'll want to skip those.)

BE FLEXIBLE WHEN ENTERTAINING

I could probably write a whole other book on just this subject, but for now, always keep in mind that everyone is a little different and try to keep your environment set up for this.

MUSIC

Put on some good music that's just background and universal. For fun, I've provided a bunch of music pairing suggestions throughout the book.

LIGHTING

Soft lighting is always best.

DRINKS

A well-stocked bar is essential. Maybe think up a suggested cocktail that reflects your theme for the night.

THINK OUTSIDE THE BOX

For example, I don't smoke cigarettes, but I always keep an ashtray outside for guests just in case.

When your guests are comfortable, you can be comfortable too, and then the party just happens.

TABLE OF CONTENTS

ff, Rosie's brother. Rosie's parents are very
their son, Jeff, who worked the coffee shop
s, was still living in Fl...
is painting and...
e. Having seen...
t say, Jeff is the...
He really is a ch...
with a pretty wom...
ssing a beat. Rosi...
with him. No ma...
and keep a smile...
ncredible speed. W...

Ashevi...

Jericho

ONE TRIBE FRIDAY OCTOBER 22nd ASHEVILLE, NC

SURSEE dreamsicle
XIST asheville collective
DAMIEN starseed
ONE NAME life, dcm
JERICHO php, astral lab

LOCATION: in the basement of HAVANA
115 Broadway, Downtown Asheville, NC
PRICE: 6 dollars
18 and up
21 to drink
doors open at 11pm

INFOLINES:
Pale Horse 828.670.6...
Astral Lab 828.252.7...
Havana   828.250...

...ed chopped fresh cilantro
/4 cup sliced jalapeño peppers

Max & Rosie's
Most
Excellent
Café &
Juice
Bar

...ive oil

...negar

...black pepper

..., cilantro, and jalapeño peppers in a foo...
e. Place in a bowl with the tomatoes.
...negar. Mix well and season with salt and
...ing.

vegetarian oasis in the heart of downtown asheville

XIV   Traveling with Jericho

ASHVILLE North Carolina

PART 1: 1998-2004

Back in '94, when I was just fourteen—and well before I started my cooking career—I did a quick stint in Highlands, North Carolina, with my uncle Joe. There I spent a couple days scrubbing pots and cleaning shrimp, then moved back to New Jersey shortly after. My stay in Highlands was brief, but I'll never forget the first time I saw my uncle cook in a professional kitchen.

I started my first official kitchen job in early '97, washing dishes somewhere in eastern Tennessee. (I moved around a lot in my younger days.) When I moved to Asheville for the first time in '98, I found work at a place called Havana's (now Broadways). I started as a dishwasher, eventually did some prep work, then began cooking on the line close to the end of my time there. I really had no idea what I was doing, but the owner seemed to like my work ethic, and I wasn't scared to dive in when needed.

At Havana's, I met some friends I still see frequently and consider lifelong mates. Caroline, the restaurant's owner, liked me enough to let me throw underground DJ shows in the basement where, eventually, that part of my life took off as well.

Havana's was a Cuban-style restaurant. I loved the ingredients they used and eventually developed my first real recipe based off of the flavors that I still enjoy so much. The recipe was published in a cookbook for a place just down the street: Max & Rosie's. My dear old friend Jeff, who has since passed on, had introduced me to his sister Rosie, and for a brief time, I worked at both restaurants, gaining valuable experience that would launch my career.

FOOD TUNES: CUBAN MUSIC

Personally, I love Buena Vista Social Club. They play real, great Cuban music, and they're a band I'll never forget from my days spent working at Havana's restaurant in Asheville.

CUBAN-STYLE ROASTED PORK

Prep time: 20 minutes
Cook time: 1 hour
Servings: 10

This is a recipe I started making at one of my first jobs as a young line cook in the late '90s, but a version of this also helped me land one of my first serious jobs as a chef in Chicago. I originally got the idea and flavor profiles for this pork roast at a Cuban restaurant where I was working, washing dishes, and doing some prep work—Havana's in Asheville. This is my "adult" version that can also be used as the base for a great Cuban sandwich.

INGREDIENTS
5 lbs. pork loin whole, cleaned and patted dry
1 Tbs. salt
2 tsp. black pepper
1 pineapple, peeled and roughly chopped
  (Save the rind!)
1 bunch fresh cilantro, roughly chopped
1 onion, cleaned and sliced
4 cloves garlic, smashed
1 cup white wine
2 cups stock (chicken or vegetable)
2 tsp. salt
2 tsp. cumin
1 tsp. cayenne pepper

TOOLS
- Dutch oven or other large, deep roasting pan
- Large skillet or sauté pan
- Meat thermometer

DIRECTIONS
1. Preheat oven to 325 degrees.
2. Take your cleaned, patted dry pork loin and rub with salt and pepper. Let rest while getting everything else together.
3. Clean your pineapple, saving the rinds, and rough chop about ¼ for cooking. (Save the rest for snacking on while you're cooking.)
4. In a large skillet or sauté pan, sear pork loin until brown and slightly caramelized on all sides.
5. Transfer to large baking pan or Dutch oven.
6. Add onions, garlic, chopped cilantro, chopped pineapple, wine, and stock.
7. Lay pineapple rinds on top of pork and cover with foil.
8. Bake in oven for 1 hour until internal temperature is around 145 degrees.
9. Let rest for 20 minutes.
10. Slice and serve!

FOOD TUNES
"Murmullo" by
Buena Vista Social Club

SPANISH BLACK BEANS

Prep time: Overnight
Cook time: 1 hour
Servings: 6-8

Beans have become one of my favorite things to cook these days. It definitely took me some time to catch on to why beans are so important to the diet, and I learned they can be incredibly tasty with a little finesse. Black beans are my daughter's and wife's favorite to eat and something that I cook on a regular basis for guests in my home and at work. Here is a simple Spanish style. Please explore the world of beans and legumes and use this as a base recipe that you can interchange with the bean of your choice. Also, always feel free to cook some extras for leftovers or to throw into the freezer for a quick meal down the road.

INGREDIENTS
4 cups dry black beans
1 medium yellow onion, roughly chopped
3 cloves garlic, smashed
1 medium carrot, sliced lengthwise
1 stalk celery, sliced lengthwise
2 bay leaves
1 ½ Tbs. kosher salt
2 tsp. black pepper
1 tsp. cayenne pepper
2 tsp. cumin
2 tsp. coriander
1 tsp. chili powder
1 Tbs. dry oregano
8 cups water or stock (Stock adds more flavor but is not necessary.)

TOOLS
- Large pot
- Strainer

DIRECTIONS
1. Cover beans completely with water and soak them overnight.
2. Drain your beans.
3. Simmer beans in 8 cups of water or stock with onion, garlic, carrot, celery, and bay leaves for about 45 minutes.
4. Once slightly tender, add spices and cook for 10-15 more minutes.
5. Finish with salt and remove from heat, but keep stirring until cool.
6. Serve and eat.

Special Notes
* To soak or not to soak ... I definitely believe that soaking beans ahead of time helps with cooking time and overall tenderness, but if you forget to do it the night before, no worries. There is hope! That being said if you choose to soak, cover completely with water in the pot you are going to cook them in for 2-24 hours.
** Stock will add more flavor but is not necessary.

FOOD TUNES
"Chan Chan" by
Buena Vista Social Club

JERICHO SALSA 2.0

Prep time: 20 minutes
Servings: 4

I know it seems a little egotistical naming a salsa after myself, but I technically didn't name this one! This is a second version of the first recipe I ever made, and the original was my first recipe ever published. I was around twenty-one years old and working at Max & Rosie's. This was a simple salsa I started working on at Havana's but took with me to Max & Rosie's. They liked it enough to add it on their menu at the time and eventually added it in their cookbook! When they asked me what to call it, I was a deer in headlights, and I just said Jericho Salsa. Here is my 2.0 version. This salsa would compliment the pork recipe from earlier or stand alone with some fresh fried tortillas.

INGREDIENTS

10 large Roma tomatoes, washed and
  medium diced
1 bunch fresh cilantro, chopped fine
1 cup red onion, diced
3 Tbs. minced jalapeño
3 cloves garlic, smashed and minced fine
½ cup apple cider vinegar
½ cup olive oil
2 tsp. kosher salt
2 tsp. black pepper
2 tsp. ground cumin
1 tsp. ground coriander
Pinch of cayenne pepper (If you like it with a
  little more kick!)

TOOLS
· Knife
· Cutting board
· Bowl

FOOD TUNES
"La Bayamesa" by
Buena Vista Social Club

DIRECTIONS
1. Chop tomatoes, onions, jalapeños, and garlic and place into a large mixing bowl.
2. Add cilantro, oil, vinegar, salt, pepper, and spices and gently mix everything well.
3. Let sit for 20 minutes to marinate and then serve!

PEEL-AND-EAT POACHED SHRIMP WITH JOANNE'S BEST COCKTAIL SAUCE

Prep time: 15 minutes
Cook time: 5 minutes
Servings: 4

This is an ode to one of my first kitchen jobs in Highlands, North Carolina. I was very young and just helping my uncle Joe, who was a chef at an Italian restaurant in the small mountain resort town. The only thing I remember doing at this short and very early stint in my culinary adventures was peeling shrimp and scrubbing giant pots and pans! (But hey, you gotta start somewhere!) It's also a cocktail sauce similar to the one my aunt Joanne makes at family get-togethers, and she is also a chef. It runs in the family, but we will get to that later. These are my latest versions of two family favorites.

INGREDIENTS
2 lbs. fresh tiger shrimp (16–20 ct. or whatever prawns you prefer)
2 lemons, one cut in half, the other juiced and zested
1 Tbs. fresh peppercorns
3 bay leaves
1 Tbs. kosher salt
2 cups ketchup
1 Tbs. Worcestershire sauce
1 Tbs. prepared horseradish
1 tsp. salt
2 tsp. Tabasco® sauce

TOOLS
• Medium pot
• Strainer
• Baking sheet
• 1 large bowl
• 1 small bowl

DIRECTIONS
The shrimp
1. In a medium pot filled with water, add one lemon cut in halves, peppercorns, bay leaves, and kosher salt and bring it to a soft boil.
2. Toss shrimp in the pot and cook for 5 minutes until shrimp are opaque and cooked through.
3. Strain immediately and lay out evenly onto a baking sheet to cool.
4. Refrigerate for 1 hour before serving.
5. Serve shrimp in a large bowl over ice and peel and eat!

The sauce
1. Mix the juice and zest of 1 lemon, ketchup, Worcestershire sauce, horseradish, salt, and Tabasco sauce in a small mixing bowl.
2. Transfer to a small bowl for serving.

FOOD TUNES
"¿Y Tú Qué Has Hecho?" by Buena Vista Social Club

ROASTED CORN ON THE COB WITH CHILI-LIME COMPOUND BUTTER

Prep time: 5 minutes
Cook time: 20-25 minutes
Servings: 6

This is a great summertime addition to any picnic or barbecue. You can grill the corn right on the grill if you want, but this recipe is oven roasted. A simple compound butter is a great finishing touch for grilled or roasted corn, and you can easily change up the ingredients to your liking for different butter flavor profiles. We are going to stick with some Latin flavors for this recipe.

INGREDIENTS

6 ears fresh corn with husk on
2 sticks unsalted butter, softened (Do not heat; just let come to room temperature.)
1 lime, zested and juiced
2 tsp. kosher salt
1 tsp. black pepper
1 large jalapeño, whole
1 tsp. chili powder

TOOLS

- Baking sheet
- Medium mixing bowl

DIRECTIONS

1. Preheat oven to 375 degrees.
2. Leaving the husk on, roast corn in oven on a baking sheet for 20-25 minutes until kernels are just tender. For the jalapeño, roast on baking sheet with corn off to the side but on the same pan.
3. Once the jalapeño is cool to the touch, deseed, discard stem, and dice small.
4. While corn is cooling before husking it, hand mix the butter, lime zest and juice, spices, and diced, roasted jalapeño in a medium mixing bowl.
5. Husk corn and top with butter compound, or toss the corn in the butter compound and then serve.

FOOD TUNES
"Dos Gardenias" by
Buena Vista Social Club

FOOD TUNES
"Amor de loca juventud"
by Buena Vista Social Club

JOANNE'S WORLD FAMOUS MOJITOS

Prep time: 5 minutes
Servings: 1 cocktail

INGREDIENTS
6-10 fresh mint leaves
4 fresh lime wedges
1 fluid oz. simple syrup
1.5 fluid oz. rum (bartender's choice)
Club soda
Ice

TOOLS
- Muddler
- Shaker
- 16 oz. glass

DIRECTIONS
1. Muddle mint leaves, lime wedges, and syrup and shake.
2. Add rum and ice cubes and shake.
3. Top with club soda.
4. Serve in a 16oz. glass and chill.

SUMMER IN HAVANA BEERTAIL

Prep time: 5 minutes
Servings: 1 cocktail

This is a very refreshing beertail using fresh watermelon juice. If you don't feel like making homemade, you can find bottled watermelon juice in specialty grocery stores, especially when in season in late summer.

INGREDIENTS
12 oz. your favorite lager or Cerveza Cristal®
 (Cuban beer) if you can find it
½ oz. fresh orange juice
1 oz. fresh pineapple juice
1 oz. fresh watermelon juice
1 oz. white rum
Ice

TOOLS
- Shaker
- Pint glass

DIRECTIONS
1. Mix all ingredients into a shaker with ice except beer.
2. Strain into a pint glass and top with cold beer.
3. Garnish with orange twist.

FOOD TUNES
"De Camino a la Vereda"
by Buena Vista Social Club

My short time living in Key West was like a long vacation with no days off. I had made my way down from Asheville, thinking island life was what I needed. I was twenty-two years old and just starting to get my chops on the line. Plus, I had some family living in Key West at the time, so I loaded up my records, clothes, and my soon-to-be famous salsa recipe.

My aunt Sue owned the famous Duval Street candy store called Key West Candy Company. It was a great, old-style candy shop, and being that I have the "Michel sweet tooth," as I've been told my whole life, I loved eating lots of free candy. I got to spend a day with Sue on one of my half days off, learning how to make fudge. There is definitely a science to all of it, and I really learned to respect my sweets a little more after this lesson.

I had another aunt, Joanne, who owned and operated the famous Dorothy's Deli on Simonton Street just a couple blocks away from Sue's place. This was where I spent most of my mornings and afternoons while living in Key West. At Dorothy's, I learned the art of the

FOOD TUNES: YACHT ROCK MIX

From Toto to Steely Dan, I'll always remember the great rock tunes I heard playing in tourist spots around Key West and, of course, some reggae—I was in the islands, after all!

KEY WEST

Florida
2002

sandwich, how to deliver lunches on a scooter, what drag comedy was (that's a whole other story), and that my family members are tough cookies to work with and for. I gained a lot of respect for both of my aunts while living and working with them. These experiences made me feel like I was truly part of a bloodline cut out for food and business.

I also met some folks right down the street on Simonton at a place called Sugar Apple Organic Café and Market. It was a vegetarian restaurant, and I was vegetarian at the time, so I really enjoyed working there. I was only working four or five days a week at Dorothy's, so I filled in at Sugar Apple a few days a week doing prep work and cooking for the lunch rush. I took pleasure in learning some tricks for my soup and lasagna prep. Tina, one of the owners, taught me the importance of the basics in a soup: a proper mirepoix (a fancy, French word for carrots, onions, and celery)—the foundation to a proper soup or sauce—and how to build from there to create any soup I ever wanted. And boy do I still use that today. I learned how to make vegan ricotta cheese and how to cook tofu properly as well.

Tina also taught me a trick I don't really use due to sanitation rules these days, but it was something I'll never forget. Her grandmother used to stick her finger in the sauce (sometimes

called "gravy," depending on where you grew up) to add love to the dish. Adding love! I've thought about that more and more as I've continued to cook for well over twenty years now. I discovered then and there that I love to cook.

My nightlife in Key West was a whole other story. I worked as a DJ—yes, the art of playing records. It was still vinyl then—actual records—and I was playing about two to four times per week with my friend Chris, who had moved down there with me. It was a lot of fun, and we made some money as well. In fact, I could write a book about my life as a DJ!

I lived in Key West with a couple guys who are still two of my best friends today. Chris, who I had met back at Havana's in Asheville, let me talk him into moving to the islands along with our buddy Alex, who I'd met through Asheville's music circuit. Funny thing is, after I'd convinced both of them to move down there, I only stayed for less than a year while Alex stayed for about three years, and Chris stayed for almost ten years! I think I just wanted to see and cook more than island life had to offer. It worked out for those guys though.

I still love Key West and try to make it down there to visit every few years. It is truly a magical place and will always hold a special place in my heart—and my palate.

FOOD TUNES
"Rosanna" by Toto

TINA'S LASAGNA

Prep time: 20 minutes
Cook time: 1 hour
Servings: 6

I met Tina while living in Key West. She is one of the owners of a fabulous health-food and deli spot right down the street from my aunt's deli, Dorothy's, on Simonton Street. I started out as a customer, grabbing supplements and smoothies after work. I eventually wound up working in the deli for Tina and her husband, Phil. Tina gave me my first lesson in true Italian cooking. She was from Philly. Small world. She always cooked with love and happiness and made me realize that cooking with passion always makes the food taste better. This is a version of the lasagna I came up with, thinking of Sugar Apple and their little health-food paradise in paradise.

INGREDIENTS

1 16-oz. pack lasagna noodles,
  ready-to-bake style*
2 jars tomato sauce
1 15 oz. tub ricotta cheese
1 large egg
1 lb. mixed wild mushrooms, cleaned and
  diced medium
1 cup red onion, sliced
3 cloves garlic, smashed
2 cups kale, julienned
1 eggplant, peeled and diced medium
4 cups mozzarella cheese, shredded
½ cup Romano cheese, grated
1 ½ Tbs. kosher salt
2 tsp. black pepper
2 tsp. oregano
1 tsp. thyme
2 tsp. crushed red pepper
1 cup Italian parsley, chopped

TOOLS

• Large sauté pan
• Large mixing bowl
• 12" x 16" glass baking dish

Special Notes
* Gluten-free noodles work just fine for this recipe.
  That's how we make it at home these days.
** Now, it's time to build your lasagna!

DIRECTIONS

1. Preheat oven to 350 degrees.
2. In large sauté pan, cook onion, mushrooms, garlic, eggplant, and kale until cooked through.
3. Season with ½ Tbs. salt and 1 tsp. black pepper.
4. Cool and reserve.
5. In large mixing bowl, add ricotta cheese, egg, the remaining salt, pepper, oregano, thyme, crushed red pepper, and parsley along with 1 cup of the mozzarella cheese.
6. Mix all ingredients well.**
7. Add half of one jar of sauce in the base of 12" x 16" dish.
8. Add 3–5 noodles.***
9. Spread ⅓ ricotta mix, then ⅓ veggie mix, then sauce over noodles.
10. Repeat layering until out of noodles, cheese mix, and veggies.
11. The top final layer is the last of the sauce, 3 cups mozzarella, and parmesan on top.
12. Bake for 1 hour until cheese is melted and internal temperature is 140 degrees.
13. Serve.****

*** It depends how many noodles you have and how big they are.
  Count your noodles out and divide as evenly as you can by three.
**** This goes great with crusty bread (or Gluten Free bread) and a
  mixed green salad. Don't forget the love!

WHITE BALSAMIC VINAIGRETTE

Prep time: 10 minutes
Servings: 6-8

O nce I figured out the basics of making a good vinaigrette, it was truly hard to buy one at the store. I hope this recipe does the same for you. In this particular recipe, we are going to use white balsamic vinegar, but you can substitute it with any vinegar you have lying around, or if you just prefer a specific type, go for it!

INGREDIENTS
1 cup white balsamic vinegar
¼ cup water
1 ½ cup olive oil
1 shallot, roughly chopped
2 cloves garlic, smashed
4 Tbs. Dijon mustard
1 Tbs. salt
1 tsp. black pepper
1 tsp. oregano

TOOLS
• Blender

DIRECTIONS
1. Add all ingredients into blender except the oil.
2. Blend well for 45 seconds.
3. Slowly drizzle oil in so it emulsifies.
4. Toss with some arugula, grape tomatoes, and bell peppers and serve.

Special Notes
You can blend this a couple ways depending on what equipment you have. My preferred way of making vinaigrettes is in a blender. You can use this same technique with a food processor or a hand mixer and the blender vessel that usually comes with it.

FOOD TUNES
"Kiss on My List"
by Hall & Oates

MY JÄGER® DAYS ARE FINALLY OVER

Prep time: 5 minutes
Servings: 1

I feel like everyone has some drink skeletons in their closet and mine is Jägermeister®. This digestif was very trendy in the late '90s ... or until I stopped drinking it, I believe. Crispy, a good friend I lived with down in Key West, believes he came up with the Jäger® bomb, and hey—anything was possible in those days. I wanted to get a little more creative with a recipe dedicated to my Jäger days other than just a shot with Red Bull®. I finally ended my Jäger tradition with my brother, Andrew, two Thanksgivings ago. He was definitely one of my Jäger buds when I was in my twenties as well. So this is what I came up with. Prost!

INGREDIENTS
1 ½ fluid oz. Jägermeister
½ lemon, juiced
Lemon slice
Sprig of rosemary
2 dash of bitters
2 Tbs. cherry juice
Ice

TOOLS
• Shaker
• Rocks glass

DIRECTIONS
1. Add all ingredients except fresh rosemary in shaker with ice.
2. Shake well.
3. Pour in rocks glass and garnish with rosemary and lemon slice.

FOOD TUNES
"Sailing"
by Christopher Cross

ISLAND-GRILLED TOMATO BISQUE

Prep time: 45 minutes
Cook time: 45 minutes
Servings: 4-6

Everyone needs a good tomato soup recipe, and this is one I have been working on for quite some time. Tina, from the Sugar Apple in Key West, gave me some basic soup techniques that I have been using for almost twenty years now. A good, basic mirepoix, clean stock, and fresh ingredients. Her mother used to stick her finger in her soups to add the love. I use a spoon instead of my finger these days, but I always add some love! This is a great comfort food addition for island life or up in the mountains on a cold winter Sunday.

INGREDIENTS
2 cups celery, roughly chopped with leaves
1 large yellow onion, roughly chopped
3 large carrots, roughly chopped
4 cloves garlic, smashed
6 large beefsteak tomatoes*
2 large red bell peppers**
1 large can whole tomatoes***
1 small can tomato juice or V8® juice, single serve
¼ cup olive oil
½ cup white wine
1 qt. water or stock (unsalted)
1 ½ Tbs. kosher salt
2 tsp. black pepper
2 tsp. paprika
2 tsp. ground fennel
1 cup parsley, chopped
1 cup fresh basil

TOOLS
- Baking sheet or grill
- Large pot
- Hand blender

DIRECTIONS
1. Grill or roast the tomatoes and peppers. Once cooked, clean the tomatoes and peppers. (Cleaning them post cooking helps to preserve more flavor from the seeds and flesh.) Then, set aside for next steps.
2. In large pot, add oil and bring up to a medium/high heat; add carrots, onions, celery, and garlic and caramelize for 8-10 minutes until fragrant.
3. Add salt, pepper, paprika, and fennel.
4. Deglaze with white wine and cook for 5 minutes.
5. Add canned tomatoes, grilled peppers and tomatoes, stock or water and simmer for 30-45 minutes on low/medium heat.
6. Finish with basil and parsley and blend with a hand blender until smooth.
7. Season with salt and pepper to taste.
8. Serve with some fresh focaccia if you have some!

Special Notes
Tossed in oil, salt, and pepper and grilled until tender through or roasted in the oven at 350 degrees for 25 minutes.
** Tossed in oil, salt, and pepper, grilled or roasted with the tomatoes.
*** Italian style preferred!

FOOD TUNES
"Hey Nineteen"
by Steely Dan

MY DOROTHY'S CUBAN-STYLE SANDWICH

Prep time: 10 minutes
Cook time: 5 minutes
Servings: 4

I never really thought of sandwich-making as an art form until I spent some time working at my aunt Joanne's deli in Key West called Dorothy's. She owned a great neighborhood spot a block off the famous Duval Street strip. I really enjoyed my time working there, making sammies, stocking beer, and delivering orders on my "racing" scooter I had while living on the island. Joanne definitely helped me become a chef. She is very organized and disciplined, and I still stand by some of her lessons today in my kitchens. I also got to spend some time with my first comedy drag queen and still my favorite, AJ, who also worked at the deli with us.

INGREDIENTS
4 Cuban-style hoagie rolls or a full Cuban loaf
1 lb. Black Forest ham
1 lb. roasted pork, thin sliced (Cuban Pork recipe on page 15)*
8 slices Swiss cheese
4 Tbs. yellow mustard
8 bread and butter deli-sliced pickles
Kosher salt
Black pepper
4 Tbs. butter

TOOLS
• Griddle or large, heavy sauté pan
• Baking sheet

DIRECTIONS
1. Slice hoagie rolls.
2. Spread mustard on both sides of each hoagie.
3. Add ham to hoagie roll bottom.
4. Add sliced pork.
5. Add pickles.
6. Top with cheese and hoagie roll top.**
7. Heat up griddle/sauté pan and melt butter.
8. Cook sammies while using baking sheet to press flat.
9. Cook on both sides until golden brown.
10. Slice on the bias (diagonally).
11. Serve immediately.

Special Notes
Grocery precooked sliced pork will work just fine!
** ¼ pound of each meat on each sammie. It will be a full meal!*

FOOD TUNES
"What a Fool Believes"
by The Doobie Brothers

KEY LIME FUDGE

Prep time: 20 minutes
Cook time: 15–20 minutes
Servings: 6

All right, so as you read from the story on page 10, my aunt Sue takes her fudge seriously. I got to make it with her once in the shop in Key West. I'll never forget that. I did my best to come up with a recipe that is close to her perfection and uses most of the same ingredients.

INGREDIENTS

3 cups sugar
16 Tbs. butter
⅔ cup evaporated milk
12 oz. white chocolate chips
7 oz. marshmallow cream
1 tsp. vanilla
½ tsp. almond extract
2 Tbs. key lime juice
½ lime, zested

TOOLS

- 9" x 13" baking pan
- Cooking spray
- Medium, heavy saucepan
- Candy thermometer

DIRECTIONS

1. Lightly spray 9" x 13" baking pan.
2. On medium heat in medium, heavy saucepan, melt butter, sugar, and evaporated milk.
3. Place a candy thermometer in saucepan, making sure the tip does not touch the bottom of pan but is submerged in fudge mixture.
4. Heat sugar, butter, and evaporated milk until there seems to be no texture.
5. Once mixture reaches 234 degrees, remove from heat.
6. Mix in white chocolate chips and stir until melted completely.
7. Mix in marshmallow cream and vanilla.
8. Pour into baking dish.
9. Chill for 24 hours before serving.

FOOD TUNES
"I Keep Forgettin'"
by Michael McDonald

SOUTHERNMOST COFFEE

Prep time: 5 minutes
Servings: 1

INGREDIENTS

1 ½ fluid oz. dark rum
½ fluid oz. orange liqueur
1 double shot espresso
1 Tbs. orange zest
½ fluid oz. agave
Ice
Splash of half and half

TOOLS

- Shaker
- Stemless martini glass

DIRECTIONS

1. Add all ingredients into a shaker with ice.
2. Shake well and strain into a stemless martini glass.

Battery Park Av

Battery Park Ave

DO NOT
BLOCK
INTERSECTION

College St

NO
TURN
ON RED

ASHEVILLE
North Carolina

PART 2: 2003-2004

Key West was just a short stint in my life, but one I will always cherish. As you may have gathered, the mountains have always called to me, so after leaving Key West, I returned to Asheville—a small town with big flavors.

I went back to Max & Rosie's for a while, but the business eventually sold. As a result, I moved up the street to Laughing Seed Café, another Asheville vegetarian staple that is still running today. (In fact, I've returned to Laughing Seed and work there now, but I'll get to that in a later chapter.) That's when I met Joan, the restaurant's owner, who still works on the line sometimes. At that point, I started to take cooking and technique a little more seriously and realized being a chef might be my second calling—along with DJ'ing, of course. I soon discovered I was pretty fast on the cafés high-volume line, and I'll never forget Marlene, who taught me how to run a window properly. I still see her occasionally these days as well.

At Laughing Seed, I learned the art of brunch but also quickly realized that I am not a Sunday morning guy. I like to DJ on Saturday nights and have family and football time on Sundays. (The latter is a tradition that was embedded into me as a young child.) So, to this day, Sunday morning is my most hated shift. Still, a delicious brunch is something every chef should have in their toolbox. After all, Americans love Benedicts and mimosas ... me included!

FOOD TUNES: '80S POP

Prince, New Order, Bowie ... I love them! This was a confusing part of my life as I tried to decide if I was more of a chef or a DJ (or maybe a little bit of both). So of course, '80s pop comes to mind; I was trying to figure things out, just like these artists were.

JACKFRUIT "CRAB CAKE" WITH BLENDER HOLLANDAISE SAUCE

Prep time: 15 minutes
Cook time: 30 minutes
Servings: 8

Brunch to me is more of an event than just a meal. Most people who work in kitchens are not fans of working these shifts, knowing that they become entertainers for the day, not just cooks. On the other hand, I love to throw a brunch event at home on nice summer days whenever I can. This recipe is a vegetarian take on a crab cake that I came up with alongside a friend, Parker. He is an enthusiast of living on the edge with creative vegetarian fare. I promise you will not know the difference between this jackfruit version and my Sunday crab cake. You can serve this on a store-bought English muffin or alone with the hollandaise sauce that follows.

INGREDIENTS
2 20-oz. cans of jackfruit in brine
2 eggs
1 medium red bell pepper, finely diced
¼ of a red onion, finely diced
juice of ½ a lemon
⅛ cup fine nori flakes (added to give jackfruit essence of the sea)
1 ¼ cups panko bread crumbs
1 tsp. kosher salt
1 tsp. black pepper
Corn meal for dusting
1 Tbs. butter
1 Tbs. cooking oil for sautéing

TOOLS
• Cooking sheet
• Medium mixing bowl
• Cast-iron skillet or heavy pan

DIRECTIONS
1. Preheat the oven to 225 degrees for "braising."
2. "Braise" the jack fruit in the oven for about 30 minutes. Once cool enough to handle, pull apart by hand and reserve.
3. Add jackfruit, eggs, red bell pepper, red onion, lemon, nori flake, panko bread crumbs, kosher salt, and pepper into a medium size mixing bowl and mix well by hand.
4. Form mixture into medium-sized patties.
5. In a heavy pan or skillet, heat up butter and oil together until sizzling.
6. Cook cakes on medium heat until golden brown on both sides.
7. You can reserve in the oven on warm or serve right away.

Special Notes
I usually get about eight medium-sized cakes. You can always use this recipe for hors d'oeuvres and just make mini versions as well.

FOOD TUNES
"Purple Rain" by Prince

BLENDER HOLLANDAISE SAUCE

Prep time: 5 minutes
Servings: 4

No one I've ever met nails hollandaise on their first try. This recipe is for all the first-timers. This is a fail-safe sauce and takes no time at all to throw together. You can take this base and go a thousand different directions by adding some Cajun spice, fresh cilantro, or just about any ingredient to help kick your brunch menu up a bit.

INGREDIENTS
3 large egg yolks
1 Tbs. fresh lemon juice
½ tsp. salt
Pinch of cayenne
Dash of Tabasco®
8 Tbs. melted butter

TOOLS
• Blender

DIRECTIONS
1. Blend yolks, lemon juice, salt, cayenne, and Tabasco in blender until smooth.
2. Slowly drizzle in melted butter and serve right away.

Special Notes
You don't want to leave this sauce sitting around for too long or it will break.

MI CORAZON'S BLOODY MARIA

Prep time: 5 minutes
Servings: 1

T his is a beverage my wife discovered while we were living in Chattanooga, and it pairs well with the recipes in this chapter. We met in the late '90s during my first stint in Asheville, and we stayed friends for many years, but we got back together during my Chicago era. This is her recipe and a great change of pace from a regular vodka Bloody Mary.

INGREDIENTS
4 fluid oz. tomato juice
2 dashes Worcestershire sauce
⅛ tsp. cracked black pepper
½ lemon, juiced
1.5 fluid oz. Espolòn Reposado Tequila®
1 tsp. Valentina® hot sauce
½ tsp. celery salt
1 stalk celery, leaves attached
1-2 tsp. (to your taste) horseradish
Pickled jalapeños
Ice

TOOLS
- Pint glass
- Shaker

DIRECTIONS
1. Add tomato juice, Worcestershire sauce, black pepper, lemon juice, tequila, hot sauce, and celery salt into shaker.
2. Add horseradish to your taste.
3. Shake well.
4. Pour into a pint glass filled with ice.
5. Garnish with 1 celery stalk, leaves attached, and a couple pickled jalapeños.

Special Notes
Espolòn Reposado Tequila is my wife's favorite, you can substitute any tequila for it.

FOOD TUNES
"I Wanna Dance with Somebody (Who Loves Me)" by Whitney Houston

OVEN-ROASTED CHICKEN

Prep time: 15 minutes
Cook time: 1 hour and 15 minutes
Servings: 4–6

My wife and I always talk about how everyone should know how to cook a few basic things to be able to survive in today's world without having to eat out constantly just for nourishment. This is definitely one of those basics that should be in every home cook's toolbox. This is also a versatile recipe—just change some of your spices to match your meal plans.

INGREDIENTS
3-lb. whole chicken* (giblets and innards removed)
1 Tbs. kosher salt
2 tsp. black pepper
2 tsp. smoked paprika**
8 Tbs. unsalted butter, softened
4 sprigs fresh thyme
1 stalk celery, leaves attached
1 small onion, peeled and quartered
1 carrot, split lengthwise and cut in half
3 cloves garlic, peeled and smashed
1 cup white wine

TOOLS
• Roasting pan

DIRECTIONS
1. Preheat oven to 350 degrees.
2. Set whole chicken in roasting pan and rub with salt, pepper, and paprika.
3. Dollop 3 Tbs. butter inside the chicken cavity along with fresh thyme, carrot, onion, celery, and garlic cloves.
4. Pour white wine into bottom of roasting pan before cooking.
5. Cook uncovered for 1 hour and 15 minutes until internal temperature is 180 degrees.
6. Once internal temperature is reached, baste chicken with butter and pan drippings.
7. Let rest 30 minutes before serving.

Special Notes
Prepare your chicken in a roasting pan to avoid getting raw chicken juice all over your kitchen.
* I like to use a free-range and local chicken if available.
** Regular paprika works fine if you don't have smoked. Like I said, this can be the main-course staple for home cooks and works great for any season!

FOOD TUNES
"Under Pressure"
by David Bowie and Queen

MUSHROOM BÉCHAMEL SAUCE

Prep time: 5 minutes
Cook time: 10 minutes
Servings: 4-6

During my second stint in Asheville, I started to learn my basics as far as traditional cooking techniques. Béchamel is one of the mother sauces in traditional French cooking, which was my favorite style of cooking in my earlier cooking adventures. I always appreciated the extra steps in French cooking, and the traditional techniques are still ones I use at work and in my home every day. Here is my version of this classic, and what follows is a mushroom addition to accompany the roasted chicken (page 27) from earlier. I hope this recipe would have satisfied the great Auguste Escoffier, one of the legendary French chefs who used to cook for kings long ago, whose cookbooks I've been trying to decipher for years.

INGREDIENTS

5 Tbs. unsalted butter
¼ cup all-purpose flour
1 qt. milk
1 Tbs. kosher salt
½ tsp. white pepper
¼ tsp. grated nutmeg

TOOLS

- Heavy saucepan
- Whisk

DIRECTIONS

1. Melt butter in heavy saucepan until sizzling; whisk in flour and continue to cook over medium heat, forming a blond roux.
2. Slowly whisk in milk and continue to cook.
3. Once milk is fully incorporated, add salt, white pepper, and nutmeg.
4. Reserve sauce and move on to sautéing mushrooms in recipe that follows.

Special Notes
Do not walk away from your stove while preparing béchamel or your sauce will scorch.

SAUTÉED WILD MUSHROOMS

Prep time: 5 minutes
Cook time: 10 minutes
Servings: 4-6

Have fun here and get a mix of whatever mushrooms you can find locally, if that's an option. If not, basic cremini, portobello, or even button mushrooms (if you can't find anything else) will work.

INGREDIENTS
1 lb. wild mushrooms, roughly cut
1 shallot, minced
1 cup white wine
  (White Boudreaux is my preference!)
3-4 sprigs fresh thyme
1 tsp. kosher salt
½ tsp. black pepper
2 Tbs. unsalted butter

TOOLS
• Large, heavy sauté pan

DIRECTIONS
1. Melt butter and cook shallots in large, heavy sauté pan until translucent.
2. Add mushrooms and cook for about 5 minutes.
3. Add wine, thyme, salt, and black pepper.
4. Reduce until all liquid is almost gone.
5. Cool for about 10 minutes.
6. Add to béchamel sauce.

PAN-GRILLED SUMMER SQUASH

Prep time: 5 minutes
Cook time: 5 minutes
Servings: 4

This is a super easy and quick recipe I use at home all summer long until zucchini and yellow squash are no longer available. This is also a basic technique used for all kinds of fresh vegetables, from green beans, broccoli, and carrots to whatever is fresh and in season. This is another staple recipe for a home cook's toolbox.

INGREDIENTS

2 medium zucchini, cut lengthwise and
  large diced
2 large yellow (crookneck) squash, cut
  lengthwise and large diced
1 shallot, julienned
½ pt. grape tomatoes, whole
3 Tbs. fresh oregano, chopped
1 Tbs. kosher salt
1 ½ tsp. black pepper
½ cup olive or avocado oil*

TOOLS

• Sauté pan

DIRECTIONS

1. In a large sauté pan, heat oil for 30 seconds then add shallot and cook for a minute.
2. Add squash and tomatoes and cook for five minutes until just cooked, or al dente.
3. Serve right away with any main course.

Special Notes

* I personally love avocado oil if you can find it! It has a mild flavor and high smoke point.

This is a perfect side dish for a picnic or barbecue. No one should have to eat mushy summer squash!

FOOD TUNES
"Once in a Lifetime"
by Talking Heads

VODKA TONIC

Prep time: 5 minutes
Servings: 1

know this seems like a pretty straightforward cocktail—and it is. It's one that I drank plenty of over the years. This drink is simple and refreshing! Here is my latest interpretation of a classic.

INGREDIENTS
1 ½ oz. vodka
2 lime twists
2 dashes of bitters
Tonic water
Lime wedge for garnish
Ice

TOOLS
• Highball glass or pint glass

DIRECTIONS
1. You can build this one directly in a highball glass or make it a tall with a pint glass.
2. Add all ingredients (except lime wedge) into your glass and stir well with a bar straw.
3. Garnish with a lime wedge and enjoy!

Special Notes
I prefer to make this drink a tall in a pint glass! My new go-to version of it is without tonic water; instead I swap the tonic out for soda water.

FOOD TUNES
"Blue Monday"
by New Order

WHO WANTS
TO HEAR SUM
FREEBIRD?!

TAKE WUN DOH
PASS IDAROUND
NINEENIE BOTTLEZ

BAR TAB DJ TOUR

PREFERRED PLEAZURE

MEMBER

PLEAZURE

around the world -- one party at a ti

FOOD TUNES: BLUES MIX

I honestly did not discover blues until my
wife introduced me to it when I was almost
forty. John Lee Hooker and Aretha Franklin
were two of the first blues artists I really
got into. Once I realized that blues was
the jazz of the South, I understood why I
liked it so much!

ATLANTA Georgia

2004(ISH)

I only spent a year in Atlanta, but it provided my cooking school crash course.

While there, I worked at a place called Gourmet Perfect that created specialized diets for people trying to lose, gain, or maintain weight. Our clientele included athletes, actors, fighters, and folks wanting to eat healthy.

I honed my technical skills, working with guys who had gone to culinary school or worked in kitchens before I was born. They were great, and they were from all over—Brooklyn, Baltimore, and a few locals. They embraced me and helped me tighten my technique. Those were my first days wearing a chef's uniform, and I hated it at first, but it grew on me. As my skills increased, I appreciated the uniform more and felt like I deserved to be wearing it.

Atlanta was also where I began cooking for enjoyment at home. I was living with one of my best friends, Dan Weeks, and we would cook together about twice per week. Cooking "together" meant me asking Dan what he wanted to eat—and then cooking it. I didn't mind. It gave us an excuse to hang out and drink beer.

During my time in Atlanta, "Friendsgiving" really started to mean something to me. Getting together with friends and celebrating with each other, food, drinks, and football became a source of joy. Thanksgiving is now my favorite holiday.

At this point, I was mostly in the kitchen, either at work or home. I was in the early stages of experimenting with no boundaries, and I really got into creating recipes. I still have some of the first ones I worked on. During that productive and exciting year, I developed a recipe for homemade country gravy, cornflake fried chicken, and ranch dressing that later made it onto a Food Network show in Chicago. Still, as I picked up new tricks, I also learned to accept failure. Apparently some of my ideas weren't so great, but I was still young and new in my career.

I now respect the food scene in Atlanta way more than I did then. It's not that it wasn't great when I lived there—it definitely was—but back then, I was still learning.

After a year in Atlanta, I moved to one of the greatest food cities in the country: Chicago. I was ready for a drastic change (and just happened to be dating a girl who lived there). That move was one of the best decisions I made as a young man.

So, off I went to Chi-Town ....

Dan Weeks and I have now spent countless Thanksgivings together, building a tradition that will always be special to me and my family. I even dedicated two recipes to the guy.

FOOD TUNES
"Burning Hell"
by John Lee Hooker

FRIENDSGIVING TURKEY WITH MAPLE BRINE

Prep time: 24 hours
Cook time: 3 hours
Servings: 10

Friendsgiving has been a tradition for me for over twenty years, and now it is my and my wife's favorite time of the year. Spending a week planning and prepping for this holiday is something I begin to get giddy about every year right around Halloween. What could be better than getting together with old friends, playing music for a couple days, drinking, and eating? This is truly a chef's holiday! I could probably write a whole book just on recipes and stories based on this one day of the year, but we are gonna stick to the basics. A simple brine and cooking technique is all you need to have a highlighted centerpiece for your special day.

INGREDIENTS
10–12-lbs. turkey
2 qt. water
3 qt. ice (for shocking the brine and
   quick usage)
1 cup real maple syrup
1 lemon, cut in half
1 cup kosher salt
6 bay leaves
3 Tbs. peppercorns
13 sprigs fresh thyme
Kosher salt
Pepper
2 carrots, sliced lengthwise
2 stalks celery, leaves attached
1 onion, cleaned and quartered
2 cups fresh sage
Butter

TOOLS
• Large Pot
• Disposable cooler
• Large roasting pan

DIRECTIONS
1. In a large pot, bring water, maple syrup, lemon, kosher salt, bay leaves, peppercorns, and 3 sprigs of thyme to soft boil.
2. Remove pot from heat and shock with ice.
3. Cool completely.
4. Add turkey to cooler and submerge it in brine and fill cooler with more ice to keep cold.*
5. Brine for 12–24 hours.
6. When ready to cook turkey, preheat oven to 325 degrees.
7. Remove turkey from brine and pat dry and place in roasting pan.**
8. Discard old brine.***
9. Discard liver and reserve giblets and neck for gravy.
10. Season outside of turkey with kosher salt and pepper.
11. Fill cavity with carrots, celery, onion, 10 sprigs fresh thyme, and sage.
12. Cook for 2 hours.
13. Raise oven temperature to 425 degrees, and while waiting for it to rise, baste turkey with melted butter and pan drippings.
14. Cook at 425 degrees for another hour until internal temperature is 165 degrees.****
15. Let turkey rest for 30 minutes.*****
16. Serve.

Special Notes
* I like to use a disposable cooler for this for easy cleanup, but you can use a regular cooler if you want.
** Disposable pans work fine, but it's worth the investment to buy a nice roasting pan, even if you only use it once a year.
*** Sanitize cooler well if you didn't use a disposable one.
**** For larger birds, add 15 minutes for every added pound.
***** Enjoy a cocktail while turkey is cooling!

MACK'S CORNBREAD

Prep time: 1 hour
Cook time: 1 hour
Servings: 6–8

Here is the basic cornbread recipe my wife uses, but if you have a favorite, go for it! It won't really affect the final recipe too much as long as it isn't too sweet.

Cornbread
INGREDIENTS

1 ½ cups yellow cornmeal
½ cup all-purpose flour
1 Tbs. baking powder
1 tsp. salt
1 tsp. sugar
1 tsp. black pepper
3 Tbs. melted unsalted butter or bacon grease
1 egg
1 ¼ cup whole milk
2 Tbs. avocado or canola oil

TOOLS

• 10" cast iron skillet
• 2 mixing bowls

DIRECTIONS

1. Preheat oven to 450 degrees.
2. While oven is preheating, leave the skillet inside oven with 2 Tbs. oil in it.
3. Mix all dry ingredients in large mixing bowl and reserve.
4. Mix all wet ingredients in separate mixing bowl and reserve.
5. Once oven is preheated, combine ingredients, mix well, and pour directly into hot skillet.
6. Bake for 25 minutes.
7. Corn bread will pop out of pan easily.
8. Cool and reserve for dressing.

MACK'S CORNBREAD DRESSING

I used to be a traditional white-bread-stuffing person until my wife shared this old family recipe using cornbread. This is always a hit at Thanksgiving and my wife's personal favorite—at least around this holiday. It's a unique and Southern comfort type of stuffing. This is also one she makes every year, and I'm kicked out of the kitchen as she prepares it.

The Dressing
INGREDIENTS
3 cups of cornbread, crumbled but not too fine
4 Tbs. (half stick) butter, melted
1 tsp. dry sage
2 ½ cups zucchini and yellow squash, diced medium
1 medium onion, diced
½ red bell pepper, diced
1 cup milk
¼ cup all-purpose flour
2 carrots, grated
8 oz. sour cream
3 tsp. salt
1 tsp. black pepper
1 tsp. poultry seasoning
Fresh sage, chopped

TOOLS
- Frying pan
- Sauce pan
- Mixing bowl
- Baking dish

DIRECTIONS
1. Preheat oven to 350 degrees.
2. Sauté bell pepper and reserve.
3. Prepare 1 cup country roux by bringing milk to a simmer in a saucepan. Whisk in all-purpose flour, 1 tsp. salt, and poultry seasoning until thick roux is formed.
4. Combine all wet ingredients and then fold in remaining ingredients. Do not overmix!
5. Transfer to greased baking dish.
6. Bake for 30 minutes.
7. Garnish with chopped fresh sage.

CHOCOLATE-PECAN BOURBON PIE

Prep time: 2.5 hours
Cook time: 55 minutes
Servings: 6

have made different variations of this for years. The crust recipe here is one that can be used for any dessert that calls for a store-bought pie dough or crust, as well as for quiche, which is usually a good day-after dish to throw together. Use bourbon of your choice, but Wild Turkey® seems most fitting for this holiday treat. You can absolutely use a store-bought crust if you don't feel like going all in—just make sure you get a deep-dish size if you do.

Pâte Brisée/ Pie Crust/ Quiche Crust
INGREDIENTS
¼ cup flour
¼ tsp. kosher salt
8 Tbs. (1 stick) cold butter, diced into small cubes
¼ cup ice water

TOOLS
- Food processor
- Mixing bowl
- Plastic wrap
- Rolling pin
- Deep-dish pie pan
- Stand mixer

DIRECTIONS
1. Add flour, salt, and butter cubes to food processor and pulse the ingredients while slowly adding ice water.*
2. Dump onto a lightly floured surface and form into a dough disk.
3. Wrap in plastic and refrigerate for 1 hour.
4. Roll out on lightly floured surface to 12 inches!**
5. Transfer to deep-dish pie pan and crimp the edges for decoration.
6. Refrigerate until filling is ready to go in.

Special Notes
It will resemble panko bread crumbs.
**The size of a record!*

Chocolate Pecan Bourbon Filling
INGREDIENTS
2 cups toasted pecans, chopped (smoked if you can)
3 eggs
¾ cup dark brown sugar
⅔ cup corn syrup
1 tsp. vanilla
1 tsp. maple syrup
2 Tbs. melted butter
¼ cup bourbon
½ tsp. kosher salt
¾ cup bittersweet chocolate chips

DIRECTIONS
1. Preheat oven to 375 degrees.
2. In stand mixer add eggs, brown sugar, corn syrup, vanilla, maple syrup, melted butter, bourbon, and salt.
3. Mix on low until everything is incorporated.
4. Fold in chocolate chips and pecans.
5. Pour into prepared pie crust.
6. Bake for 55 minutes until center is set.
7. Let stand 1 hour before serving.

CRANBERRY ORANGE MARTINI

Prep time: 5 minutes
Servings: 1

Who doesn't need a couple martinis around Thanksgiving? The stress of friends and family getting together can be overwhelming, especially if you're the host. If you have a couple of these ready for your guests when they arrive, you will have a fighting chance of a calm and collected holiday. If not, just have a few more yourself!

INGREDIENTS
1 ½ oz. Beefeater® gin
1 oz. simple syrup
6 fresh cranberries
½ oz. fresh orange juice
½ oz. fresh cranberry juice
Ice
Sprig of fresh thyme for garnish

TOOLS
• Martini glass
• Shaker

DIRECTIONS
1. Muddle 4 fresh cranberries in the bottom of martini shaker.
2. Add simple syrup, gin, juices and ice to shaker.
3. Shake vigorously.
4. Strain into martini glass.
5. Garnish with fresh thyme sprig and 2 fresh cranberries

FOOD TUNES
"The Thrill Is Gone"
by B.B. King

FOOD TUNES
"Hoochie Coochie Man"
by Muddy Waters

CORNFLAKE FRIED CHICKEN

Prep time: 20 minutes
Cook time: 40 minutes

I call this my South-meets-France technique. I like to pre-poach my chicken in a simple brine. It takes the guesswork out of frying at home while trying to maintain an exact heat and making sure all your pieces of chicken are cooked thoroughly. It can be a pain without a professional fryer, so I came up with this technique.

Poached Chicken
INGREDIENTS
4 lbs. whole chicken, cut into pieces*
Water
1 onion, cleaned and halved
1 carrot, cut lengthwise
1 stalk celery, leaves attached
1 clove garlic, smashed
½ lemon
5 peppercorns
1 Tbs. salt

TOOLS
- Large pasta pot**
- Food processor
- 2 large mixing bowls
- Cast-iron skillet

DIRECTIONS
1. Fill large pot ¾ of the way with water. Add all ingredients except chicken and bring to a boil.
2. Once water is boiling, add your chicken pieces and cook at medium heat for 30 minutes until cooked through.
3. Drain and reserve chicken.

Cornflake Crust
INGREDIENTS
1 18-oz. box of cornflakes
1 cup all-purpose flour
1 ½ Tbs. kosher salt
1 Tbs. black pepper
2 Tbs. onion powder
2 Tbs. garlic powder
2 Tbs. chili powder
1 Tbs. smoked paprika
1 cup buttermilk
2 eggs
2 qt. oil

DIRECTIONS
1. Grind cornflakes in a food processor or a blender until fine like bread crumbs.
2. Mix ground flakes with flour, salt, and spices in a large mixing bowl and set aside.
3. In a large cast-iron skillet, add 2 quarts frying oil and bring up to 300 degrees.
4. In a separate large mixing bowl, mix buttermilk and eggs.
5. Create an assembly line with chicken first, buttermilk mix, and then the cornflake dredge.
6. Dip your chicken into buttermilk a couple pieces at a time, then dredge in cornflake mix and drop into skillet.
7. Fry on both sides until crispy and golden brown.
8. Hold finished pieces in warm oven while cooking the rest.
9. Serve immediately.

Special Notes
* Look for chicken already broken down and cut for you at the grocery store.
** You will need a pasta pot large enough to submerge all your chicken parts together with room for them to move around.

GEORGIA PEPPER GRAVY

Prep time: 5 minutes
Cook time: 15 minutes
Servings: 6

Y ou haven't been to the South if you haven't tasted this rich classic! It has become one of my favorite finishing touches to fried chicken or on top of biscuits. My version is simple and similar to a béchamel sauce. You can definitely add some different spices to take this to a Cajun flavor or some fresh herbs if you want to get fancy, but I like it just simple and rich. I hope this would make Paul Prudhomme proud.

INGREDIENTS
8 Tbs. butter or ½ cup bacon grease
¾ cup all-purpose flour
1 ½ tsp. kosher salt
2 tsp. black pepper
1 tsp. white pepper
4 cups milk

TOOLS
- Medium, heavy saucepot
- Whisk
- Gravy boat

DIRECTIONS
1. Melt your butter or bacon grease in saucepot and slowly whisk in flour to create a roux.
2. Add salt and both peppers and cook gently for a minute.
3. Slowly start to whisk in milk and simmer until gravy has thickened and flour has cooked through. This should take about 10 minutes.
4. Serve.

FOOD TUNES
"Ain't No Way"
by Aretha Franklin

SOUTHERN SLAW

Prep time: 15 minutes
Servings: 6-8

C oleslaw is a staple at Southern barbecues and backyard get-togethers. It's versatile as a side dish and a quick throw-together to add a final touch to a summer meal. This is one my wife makes for all of our barbecue events.

INGREDIENTS
4 cups green cabbage, shredded
1 cup purple cabbage, shredded
2 carrots, peeled and shredded
¼ yellow onion, minced
¼ cup mayonnaise
¼ cup plain yogurt
1 tsp. apple cider vinegar
1 tsp. sugar
1 tsp. Dijon mustard
2 tsp. salt
1 tsp. black pepper

TOOLS
- Large bowl

DIRECTIONS
1. Mix all ingredients in a large bowl.
2. Chill for 1 hour.
3. Serve.

THE COBRA

Prep time: 5 minutes
Servings: 1

So I had the name of this drink before I had any idea of what kind of drink it would be. The Cobra was some random way one of my best friends, Dan W., would try and annoy me during our time living together in Atlanta. Dan is a comedian, a DJ, and a good friend, but he always enjoyed pushing the buttons no one else was allowed to. Even to this day, it's the same with us. Dan came up with this recipe for us. Enjoy and make sure you say, "Here comes the cobra!" after making the cocktail every time!

INGREDIENTS
1 ½ fluid oz. bourbon
1 fluid oz. lemon juice
½ fluid oz. cinnamon syrup
Ice

TOOLS
• Shaker
• Rocks glass

DIRECTIONS
1. Add all ingredients into a shaker.
2. Shake the hell out of it and strain into a rocks glass with ice.

FOOD TUNES
"Life by the Drop"
by Stevie Ray Vaughan

RESTAURANT

MC...
...ti mac and chees...

...lt Coo...
Old

...ked black pepper... ...lls

...n Soup $9
...ock, house cro...

...orf Sala...
...ts, cit...

FOOD TUNES: KARL ALMARIA

I've been saying for years that Karl Almaria actually plays the soundtrack to my life, and he really does. For years, he has put out new music that inspires me when I'm cooking, and his music reminds me to play music more often. He plays a mix of deep, soulful, house music of all different sorts, and I listen to him constantly. (Oh yeah, and I actually know the guy too—and he likes my cooking!)

CHICAGO
Illinois
2005-2010

Upon my arrival in Chicago, I was ready for some serious cooking. My time in Atlanta had prepared me for the next big step in my career. In this great city, I met Dan Smith and Steve McDonagh, the Hearty Boys. At the time, they had a cooking show on the Food Network called "Party Line with the Hearty Boys." I believe they were getting ready to film their second season when we met.

They graciously took me in as their executive chef for the catering department. They also had a restaurant called HB on Halsted Street in the Boystown neighborhood. I spent the next five years with the Hearty Boys. I learned more about food and how to cook during this time than at any other point in my culinary life.

During my time in Chicago, I lived in a couple different spots within the city and spent time in the many cultured neighborhoods it has to offer. Each had its own great places to eat as well as markets I still brag about today.

I spent almost three years in Lakeview, which was just a few blocks from Wrigley Field. Man, I could write a whole other book on the late nights I spent on Clark Street, going to clubs and grabbing late-night eats. I spent the last two years living in Uptown. There was also a small strip called Little Vietnam, which was where I did most of my grocery shopping.

I fell in love with the city of Chicago and searched the city high and low for new ingredients, meeting chefs of all calibers. Dan truly took me under his wing and encouraged me to try new things and not fear experimenting with my own cooking. I learned my own palate and what it was capable of. I discovered the art of buffet design and wedding planning and actually had a knack for it.

The excitement of running a full-service catering company—in one of the greatest cities in the world—with two guys who had a TV show on Food Network was definitely a high point in my career, and I was overwhelmed with feelings of accomplishment.

I also met my good friend Jon Carl when I started with the Hearty Boys. He was the chef at HB. JC made an immediate impact on me, and his food and personality were—and still are—awe-inspiring. He always said what was on his mind and said it with passion. And he was from Philly too! Every time I had a chance, I would hang out with JC, eating at HB to enjoy his incredible food or just catching up or venting about my day. HB was a bring your own bottle (BYOB) restaurant, so I always brought him a bottle of bubbles to try—if only for a single drink and a hello.

(Continued page 47)

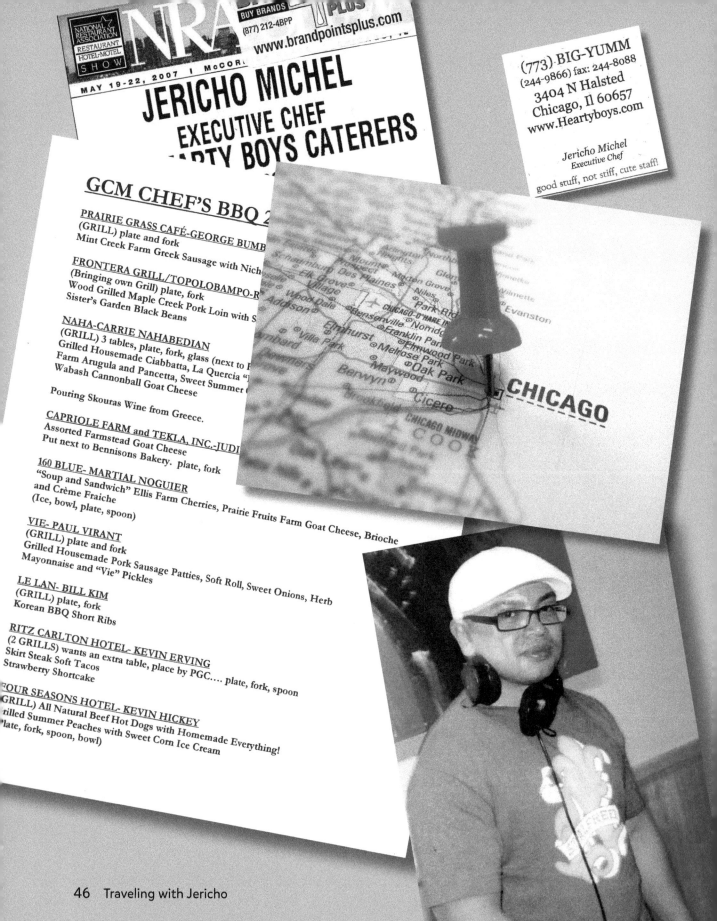

NRA

NATIONAL
RESTAURANT
ASSOCIATION
RESTAURANT
HOTEL·MOTEL
SHOW

BUY BRANDS
PLUS
(877) 212-4BPP
www.brandpointsplus.com

MAY 19-22, 2007 | McCOR

JERICHO MICHEL
EXECUTIVE CHEF
ARTY BOYS CATERERS

(773) BIG-YUMM
(244-9866) fax: 244-8088
3404 N Halsted
Chicago, Il 60657
www.Heartyboys.com

Jericho Michel
Executive Chef
good stuff, not stiff, cute staff!

GCM CHEF'S BBQ 2

PRAIRIE GRASS CAFÉ-GEORGE BUMB
(GRILL) plate and fork
Mint Creek Farm Greek Sausage with Nich

FRONTERA GRILL/TOPOLOBAMPO-R
(Bringing own Grill) plate, fork
Wood Grilled Maple Creek Pork Loin with S
Sister's Garden Black Beans

NAHA-CARRIE NAHABEDIAN
(GRILL) 3 tables, plate, fork, glass (next to
Grilled Housemade Ciabbatta, La Quercia "
Farm Arugula and Pancetta, Sweet Summer
Wabash Cannonball Goat Cheese

Pouring Skouras Wine from Greece.

CAPRIOLE FARM and TEKLA, INC.-JUDI
Assorted Farmstead Goat Cheese
Put next to Bennisons Bakery. plate, fork

160 BLUE- MARTIAL NOGUIER
"Soup and Sandwich" Ellis Farm Cherries, Prairie Fruits Farm Goat Cheese, Brioche
and Crème Fraiche
(Ice, bowl, plate, spoon)

VIE- PAUL VIRANT
(GRILL) plate and fork
Grilled Housemade Pork Sausage Patties, Soft Roll, Sweet Onions, Herb
Mayonnaise and "Vie" Pickles

LE LAN- BILL KIM
(GRILL) plate, fork
Korean BBQ Short Ribs

RITZ CARLTON HOTEL- KEVIN ERVING
(2 GRILLS) wants an extra table, place by PGC…. plate, fork, spoon
Skirt Steak Soft Tacos
Strawberry Shortcake

FOUR SEASONS HOTEL- KEVIN HICKEY
(GRILL) All Natural Beef Hot Dogs with Homemade Everything!
rilled Summer Peaches with Sweet Corn Ice Cream
late, fork, spoon, bowl)

CHICAGO

(Continued)

It took me years to understand why I was so fascinated with JC's style and technique. Now I know it's because he represents pure comfort when he presents his food; you can taste his passion and honesty in each and every plate he puts out. I realized later in life, once I was truly honest about my own dishes and relaxed while preparing them, that this was what he had already nailed years ago. It's a great feeling to discover what you represent in this crazy culinary world. I will never forget the talks, drinks, and good times I spent with JC.

I still keep in touch with JC now. After I left Chicago, he owned and operated two restaurants there, but he has since moved back to Philly, where he owns and operates two fantastic spots that truly represent his love of food. I always try to stop by when I'm in town, and I still bring a bottle of bubbles so I can lure him to my table for a chat.

I spent five years engaging in new endeavors with the Hearty Boys. In 2010, just before I made my journey back to the South, I opened a second restaurant with them called Hearty. I was heading back down after I had somehow—miraculously—reunited with Mackenzie, the love of my life, who I had dated way back in '99 during my first stint in Asheville. Fate had brought us back together when I attended a music festival she'd coordinated in North Georgia.

Before I knew it, Mackenzie and I were engaged, and I was heading to Chattanooga where I'd meet Ryan and Matt—"the guys," as I now call them—and start my new journey with the lovely woman who has helped me along in this crazy adventure called life. My wife is, has been, and will always be my rock and my inspiration.

Sure, it was hard to say goodbye to Chicago, but it won't be the last that great city will see of me.

"THE" LAMB BURGER

Prep time: 10 minutes
Cook time: 4–5 minutes
Servings: 4

This recipe followed me through a couple states, made it into a magazine or two, and still has a home on a menu in Tennessee somewhere. I guess this was my shining moment and hopefully not my only one. I remember the first version of this was an hors d'oeuvre idea for a cocktail party—a Greek meatball of sorts—with ouzo shallots and a feta crème. (Or it was something like that!) Well, after I got this onto a menu or two for events, it took off on its own and made it on brunch menus as a burger and then as a permanent staple item for a few years in different restaurants. Here is my updated version of this now-classic that has landed in my toolbox.

INGREDIENTS
1 ½ lbs. ground lamb
3 medium shallots, minced
1 clove garlic, smashed and minced
2 sprigs fresh oregano, minced
½ lemon, juiced
2 tsp. kosher salt
1 tsp. black pepper
2 tsp. dry oregano
½ tsp. cinnamon

TOOLS
- Large mixing bowl
- Frying pan or grill

DIRECTIONS
1. In a large mixing bowl, mix all ingredients by hand until well incorporated.
2. Form 4 patties and let rest for 5 minutes.
3. Pan sear or grill for 4–5 minutes until medium rare.*
4. Serve burgers on a firm, fresh bun or pita.**

Special Notes
This is my preferred cooking temperature for lamb, but you can take it further if you'd like.
**The Feta Aioli and Ouzo-Candied Shallots (page 51) are my two favorite accoutrements for this burger.*

FOOD TUNES
Karl Almaria, What Is Karl
Playing Now, Episode 067,
Mixcloud.com

ROASTED FINGERLING FRIES

Prep time: 10 minutes
Cook time: 12 minutes
Servings: 4

Fingerling potatoes are great for making roasted fries. I love a French-fried potato just as much as anyone else, but this is a great alternative, roasted in the oven and quick so you can get your potato fix. Fingerling potatoes are a cool, waxy potato and easy to cut into fry shapes, given that they are the shape and size of troll fingers.

INGREDIENTS

1 lb. fingerling potatoes, cleaned and quartered into fry shape
¼ cup avocado oil
2 cloves garlic, smashed and minced
1 Tbs. fresh oregano, chopped
1 Tbs. fresh thyme, chopped
½ Tbs. fresh rosemary, chopped
2 tsp. kosher salt
1 tsp. black pepper

TOOLS

- Large mixing bowl
- Heavy baking sheet
- Cooking spray

DIRECTIONS

1. Preheat oven to 450 degrees.
2. Toss cleaned and cut potatoes in large mixing bowl with oil, salt, garlic, oregano, thyme, pepper, and rosemary and mix well.
3. Transfer to greased heavy baking sheet.
4. Cook 10–12 minutes.*

Special Notes
Bake longer if you like them crispy!

OUZO-CANDIED SHALLOTS

Prep time: 5 minutes
Cook time: 10 minutes
Servings: 4-6

This is what really stole the show with my lamb burger at a Chicago house party when I first put that idea to work. I was learning a little bit about cocktailing and the art of the drink while catering in and around Chicago. I stumbled onto Ouzo and loved the bright licorice flavors it had. I was intrigued to cook with it, so this is what I came up with.

INGREDIENTS
8 large shallots, julienned
3 Tbs. olive oil
1 tsp. kosher salt
½ tsp. black pepper
1 Tbs. sugar
¼ cup water
¼ cup Ouzo

TOOLS
• Julienne peeler
• Medium, heavy skillet

DIRECTIONS
1. Heat medium, heavy skillet on high. Add oil and let sizzle.
2. Add shallots and return heat to medium and keep moving the pan.
3. Sauté shallots until translucent.
4. Add ¼ cup Ouzo
5. Add salt, pepper, and sugar.
6. Cook until onions are coated, then add water and reduce until water has evaporated.*

Special Notes
Onions should reach a candy-like texture.

FETA AIOLI

Prep time: 5 minutes
Servings: 6-8

I know very well most chefs will curse me for using the word "aioli" here. I am aware we have worn out this term for mayonnaise sauce in America. I am going to do my best to do this right. The true meaning of "aioli" is "garlic and oil." A French version would be "garlic mayonnaise." That's closer to what I present here, and I have used this finishing sauce so many times on menus. This sauce provides a Greek finishing touch to my lamb burger, but it can be used with any burger you like.

INGREDIENTS
1 cup mayonnaise*
½ cup feta cheese, crumbled
1 Tbs. fresh lemon juice
1 tsp. salt
½ tsp. black pepper
½ tsp. dry oregano

TOOLS
• Small mixing bowl

DIRECTIONS
1. Mix all ingredients in small mixing bowl.
2. Chill for 30 minutes before serving.

Special Notes
By all means, make it from scratch if you have the time!

CHI-TOWN CELLO

Prep time: 5 minutes
Servings: 4

This is my take on a Midwest limoncello. An easy, pitcher-style drink you can make ahead of time for a get-together at home, or something you can prep and bring to a cocktail party.

INGREDIENTS
½ cup simple syrup or agave
6 basil leaves, muddled
2 lemons, juiced*
1 bottle prosecco
Sugar

TOOLS
- Pitcher
- Muddler
- Cocktail glasses
- Small bowl
- Paper towel

DIRECTIONS
1. Muddle basil in large pitcher.
2. Add and mix lemon zest, simple syrup, lemon juice, and prosecco.
3. Serve in festive cocktail glasses with a sugar rim.**

Special Notes
* Zest one of the lemons before juicing it and add to pitcher.
** For a nice presentation and a little more sweetness to this slightly bitter but refreshing party cocktail, rub a damp paper towel along the rim of the glass. Then, dip the rim into a bowl of sugar, coating the rim.

GALLIANO® BREAD PUDDING

Prep time: 10 minutes
Cook time: 1 hour
Servings: 6

G alliano is a very cool herbal liquor that you don't see used that often. It was first created in the late 1800s and hails from Italy. It has always reminded me of bananas, so I paired it with this banana-chocolate bread pudding. It adds some nice spice notes and excitement to this basic but delicious bread pudding recipe. You can take this basic recipe and add your favorite fruits in place of the chocolate and bananas.

INGREDIENTS
4 cups brioche bread*
5 eggs
2 cups milk
1 Tbs. vanilla
3 very ripe bananas, sliced
1 cup dark chocolate chips
3 Tbs. Galliano
2 Tbs. unsalted butter

TOOLS
• 9" x 5" baking pan
• Large mixing bowl
• Large roasting pan
• Water

DIRECTIONS
1. Preheat oven to 350 degrees.
2. In a large mixing bowl, mix eggs, milk, sugar, vanilla, and Galliano until smooth.
3. Fold in bread, chocolate chips, 1 Tbs. of melted butter, and bananas.
4. Grease baking pan with 1 Tbs. of butter.
5. Transfer mixture into greased baking pan.
6. Fill a large roasting pan halfway with water creating a water bath.
7. Place the 9" x 5" pan in the water, bath.
8. Bake for 1 hour or until center has set.
9. Cool for an hour before serving.

Special Notes
* A loaf of French bread will work fine if you can't find brioche.

FOOD TUNES
Karl Almaria, What Is Karl
Playing Now, Episode 051,
Mixcloud.com

FOOD TUNES
Cocktail Party Tunes!
Karl Almaria, What Is Karl
Playing Now, Episode 028,
Mixcloud.com

"ALMOST" FAMOUS SMOKY RANCH DIP

Prep time: 10 minutes
Cook time: 1 hour
Servings: 6-8

This recipe definitely has story. I originally came up with the basic idea for this dip while in Atlanta. But it became "almost" famous while I was living in Chicago when the Hearty Boys featured a version of this recipe on Food Network! Like I said, "almost" famous. You can serve this with whatever local, seasonal veggies you have available.

INGREDIENTS
1 cup sour cream*
1 cup mayonnaise
½ cup heavy cream
1 tsp. dry oregano
1 tsp. dry basil
1 tsp. onion powder
1 tsp. garlic powder
2 ½ tsp. salt
1 tsp. black pepper
1 Tbs. smoked paprika
1 Tbs. honey or agave
¼ cup parsley, chopped fine

TOOLS
- Whisk
- Large mixing bowl

DIRECTIONS
1. Combine all ingredients and whisk well in large mixing bowl.
2. Refrigerate 1 hour before serving.

Special Notes
You can subtitute plain yogurt if you prefer it.

OUZO: "SHAKEN, NOT STIRRED"

Prep time: 5 minutes
Servings: 1

INGREDIENTS
1 fluid oz. ouzo
1 fluid oz. vodka
1 fluid oz. peach schnapps
4 muddled mint leaves
½ fluid oz. agave
Squeeze of ¼ lemon
Dash of ground cloves
Ice

TOOLS
- Muddler
- Shaker
- Martini glass

DIRECTIONS
1. Muddle mint in shaker.
2. Add remaining ingredients into shaker and shake well.
3. Strain into martini glass.
4. Garnish with lemon twist.

ROASTED SALMON DIP

Prep time: 15 minutes
Cook Time: 12-15 minutes
Servings: 4-6

Yes that says "roasted," not "smoked"! I love smoked salmon, but how many people can or will actually smoke the fish themselves at home? Maybe two out of five hundred would—I'm just saying! Anyway, I put this recipe together so you can say you made everything from scratch for whatever awesome party you are bringing this dip to.

INGREDIENTS
8-10 oz. salmon fillet, skin removed
2 Tbs. olive oil
Squirt of lemon
8 oz. cream cheese, softened
¼ cup plain Greek yogurt
¼ cup capers
1 Tbs. caper brine
2 Tbs. shallots, minced
1 Tbs. fresh dill, chopped
½ tsp. Worcestershire sauce
½ tsp. Tabasco® sauce
1 tsp. salt
½ tsp. black pepper

TOOLS
- Roasting pan
- Large mixing bowl

DIRECTIONS
1. Preheat oven to 350 degrees.
2. Place salmon on roasting pan and rub with olive oil, dash of salt, dash of pepper, and lemon.
3. Roast for 12-15 minutes cooking through.
4. Reserve and cool in fridge while making the dip.
5. Mix cream cheese, Greek yogurt, capers, caper brine, shallots, dill, Worcestershire sauce, Tabasco sauce, salt, and pepper in large mixing bowl.
6. Gently fold in 6-8 oz. of cooked and cooled salmon.
7. Refrigerate 1-2 hours before serving.

Special Notes
I typically serve this with rye crackers, shaved onions, capers, and grape tomatoes.

SAVORY CHEESECAKE

Prep time: 15 minutes
Cook time: 20-25 minutes
Servings: 6-8

This is a great cocktail party idea that most people have not heard of or thought about. Dan Smith of the Hearty Boys gave me this idea when I was a young chef in Chicago, I ran with it for years, and I had a version of this on menus all over the country for parties and weddings, or just fun get-togethers (special ones at least). Here is my basic cheesecake recipe, but remember, you can change up the flavor profile with anything you like or have available.

INGREDIENTS
3 Tbs. melted unsalted butter
1 cup panko bread crumbs*
½ cup parmesan cheese, shredded
Pinch of black pepper
16 oz. cream cheese, softened**
1 cup mascarpone cheese
4 eggs
2 tsp. salt
3 Tbs. fresh parsley, minced
1 Tbs. fresh lemon juice
½ tsp ground white pepper
1 Tbs. white truffle oil

TOOLS
- Deep-dish pie pan or springform cheesecake pan
- Small mixing bowl
- Large mixing bowl

DIRECTIONS
1. Preheat oven to 350 degrees.
2. Grease pie pan.
3. Mix melted butter, panko bread crumbs, parmesan cheese, and pepper by hand in small mixing bowl.
4. Press crust mixture into pan along bottom and slightly up sides.
5. Reserve finished crust.
6. Mix remaining ingredients well in large mixing bowl.
7. Pour cheesecake mixture into crust.
8. Bake for 20-25 minutes until center is set.
9. Cool to room temperature.
10. Refrigerate 2 hours before serving.***

Special Notes
No substitutes here!
* Philadelphia brand, of course!*
*** Serve with fresh grapes, apple, pears, and crackers.

EL GUAPOS RESTAU
requests the pleasure of your company at the

16 FRAZIER AVE
CHATTANOOGA, TN

Saturday the nineteenth of April two-thousand and fourteen

Please enjoy food on us and drink on you anytime from 6 - 9pm.

The official going away jam for Mackenzie and Jericho

Comedian
Dan Weeks   Starting the night off
                                 @ 8PM

Followed by DJ talent

DJC and
Kevin Knowell   4 deep
                    Atlanta GA

Jericho   Direct Play

Spoon
                    Jack Junkies

Festivities start at 8 pm No Cover!!

FOOD TUNES: '90S HIP HOP

You can find some great DJ mixes for '90s hip-hop—Funkmaster Flex comes to mind here! Chattanooga was far from the South Jersey neighborhood that would make the most sense here, but for some reason, I always felt a little '90s hip-hop while living there. Plus, my boss at the Terminal BrewHouse constantly sang old '90s hip-hop tunes to me. Maybe that was it ....

CRAFT BEER. CRAFTY FOOD.
Open from 11 am to 12 am 7 days
East 14th Street • Chattanooga, TN 37408
752-8090 • Fax 423-752-8092

CHATTANOOGA
Tennessee

2010-2013

Leaving my Chicago era behind, I returned to the South, where I got married and began another big part of my culinary adventure. I moved to Chattanooga, Tennessee, with no idea of what was next. I briefly worked at a kitchen called Public House before I found the Terminal BrewHouse, where I met Matt and Ryan.

Those two guys became my teachers for how to properly manage and create structure in restaurants, and they taught me a ton about beer and brewing as well. To this day, I teach and live by many of the rules I learned from them, and I cherish their wisdom and how they helped me grow into a real chef. Ryan always pushed me to try bold things in the kitchen and not forget the big picture, and he taught me how to create a real dining experience—not just good food.

With Ryan and Matt's guidance, I learned how to make hot sauce (which now has a whole story of its own in my life). I also learned curing and pickling techniques that I still use on a regular basis—both at home and in professional kitchens—and how to make homemade jerky.

I spent three years in Chattanooga before returning home to Philadelphia, but in early 2014, the guys lured me back down to open Beast + Barrel, a place I helped open from the ground up and operated for a short time before moving forward to my next adventure.

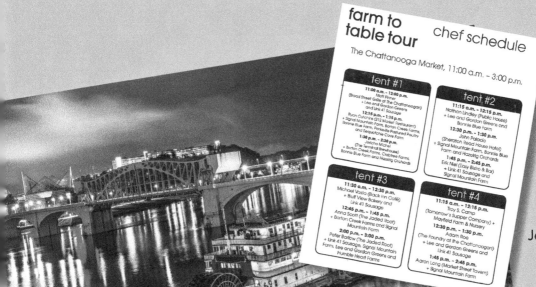

farm to table tour — chef schedule

The Chattanooga Market, 11:00 a.m. – 3:00 p.m.

tent #1

11:00 a.m. – 12:00 p.m.
Matt Pinner
(Broad Street Grille at The Chattanoogan)
+ Lee and Gordon Greens
and Link 41 Sausage

12:15 p.m. – 1:15 p.m.
Ryan Cutrohan (212 Market Restaurant)
+ Signal Mountain Farm, Boran Creek Farms,
Bonnie Blue Farm, Parksville Pastured Poultry
and Sequatchie Cove Farm

1:30 p.m. – 2:30 p.m.
Jericho Michel
(The Terminal Brewhouse)
+ Barton Creek Farm, Crabtree Farms,
Bonnie Blue Farm and Hazeltig Orchards

tent #2

11:15 a.m. – 12:15 p.m.
Nathan Lindley (Public House)
+ Lee and Gordon Greens and
Bonnie Blue Farm

12:30 p.m. – 1:30 p.m.
John Palacio
(Sheraton Read House Hotel)
+ Signal Mountain Farm, Bonnie Blue
Farm and Hazeltig Orchards

1:45 p.m. – 2:45 p.m.
Erik Niel (Easy Bistro & Bar)
+ Link 41 Sausage and
Signal Mountain Farm

tent #3

11:30 a.m. – 12:30 p.m.
Michael Vzsla (Black Inn Café)
+ Bluff View Bakery and
Link 41 Sausage

12:45 p.m. – 1:45 p.m.
Anna Scott (The Jaded Roof)
+ Barton Creek Farm and Signal
Mountain Farm

2:00 p.m. – 3:00 p.m.
Peter Barlow (The Jaded Roof)
+ Link 41 Sausage, Signal Mountain
Farm, Lee and Gordon Greens and
Humble Heart Farms

tent #4

11:15 a.m. – 12:15 p.m.
Troy S. Camp
(Tomorrow's Supper Company) +
Mayfield Farm & Nursery

12:30 p.m. – 1:30 p.m.
Adam Rice
(The Foundry at the Chattanoogan)
+ Lee and Gordon Greens and
Link 41 Sausage

1:45 p.m. – 2:45 p.m.
Aaron Long (Market Street Tavern)
+ Signal Mountain Farm

SALMON PASTRAMI

Prep time: 15 minutes
Servings: 4-6

originally found a recipe like this in an old Culinary Institute of America (CIA) textbook. I was immediately intrigued. I love homemade pastrami and making it with salmon sounded incredible. I developed this recipe for Beast + Barrel.

INGREDIENTS

3 lbs. salmon side, deboned, skin on
½ lemon, juiced
8 oz. sugar
8 oz. salt
2 Tbs. molasses
Bay leaf
Pinch of cayenne
1 cup mustard powder
1 cup garlic powder
1 cup onion powder
½ cup coriander
5 Tbs. black pepper
2 cups brown sugar
1 cup chili powder

TOOLS

- 2 small mixing bowls
- Large mixing bowl
- Cooking brush
- Large cheesecloth
- Nonperforated baking pan
- Pan
- Paper towel
- Sealed container
- Small saucepot

FOOD TUNES
Any of Funkmaster Flex's
"60 Minutes of Funk"
tapes are GREAT!

DIRECTIONS

1. Mix salt and sugar together in small bowl and reserve.
2. Brush the salmon with lemon juice.
3. Place the salmon into a large piece of cheesecloth, pack well with the salt and sugar on top, and cover completely.
4. Place onto perforated pan and refrigerate.*
5. Set and forget for 3 days!
6. After 3 days, scrape the salt-sugar cure mix off and discard. Pat dry with a paper towel.
7. Combine molasses, bay leaf, and cayenne, and heat slightly in small saucepot on stove.
8. Lightly brush molasses mix onto top of salmon.**
9. Combine mustard powder, garlic powder, onion powder, coriander, black pepper, brown sugar, and chili powder in large mixing bowl.
10. Pat pastrami spice blend onto top of salmon generously.***
11. Let rest for up to 12 hours in refrigerator.
12. When ready to serve, thinly slice salmon on the bias/at an angle and keep chilled until feeding time.

Special Notes

* *Make sure you have a nonperforated baking pan underneath salmon to catch the water as it cures!*
** *This will help the spice blend stick and also adds some depth with flavor overall.*
*** *Don't be shy with packing on the spice blend here as it is what makes this recipe so good. Reserve any remaining mix in a sealed container and use later for other recipes!*

RED PEPPER MAYONNAISE

Prep time: 5 minutes
Cook Time: 5 minutes
Servings: 4–6

This has become a favorite for me on any sandwich, and I have been making versions of this in kitchens all over. This one pairs up with the salmon pastrami from above quite well.

INGREDIENTS
1 lb. red bell peppers, whole
1 clove garlic, smashed and minced
½ cup mayonnaise
Zest of half a lemon
2 tsp. fresh lemon juice
⅛ tsp. cayenne pepper
1 tsp. salt

TOOLS
• Gas range or heavy sauté pan
• Blender
• Covered bowl
• Plastic wrap

DIRECTIONS
1. Fire roast peppers on open flame over gas stove top.*
2. Place blackened peppers in a bowl just large enough for peppers and cover with plastic wrap until cool enough to handle.
3. Once cooled, deseed peppers and discard stems.
4. Peel unwanted blackened skin from outside of peppers.
5. Blend all ingredients in blender until smooth and transfer to covered bowl.
6. Chill in refrigerator for 30 minutes before serving.

Special Notes
Fire roasting is easy and quick if you have a gas range. Simply roast directly over flame until skin has blackened. If you don't have this open-flame option, no worries! Toss peppers in 1 tsp. oil and roast in a heavy sauté pan in the oven until very soft. Let cool.

TERMINAL HOT SAUCE

Prep time: 30 minutes
Cook time: 45 minutes
Servings: 10–15

I was never a big fan of hot sauce until my wife challenged me to try a wide variety of homemade ones that were very good. I created my first one while in Chattanooga, working at the Terminal BrewHouse, but I have gotten pretty close to our perfect one over the years. This one has great body and flavor and is not just heat and vinegar. This really easy recipe is a little time-consuming to make, but it is worth it in the end, and it is great individually packaged as a holiday gift. This recipe is a refrigerated one that keeps for months, so don't worry about jarring technique here.

INGREDIENTS

10 large jalapeños, sliced with seeds
2 large yellow onions, chopped roughly
10–15 dry árbol chilis, whole*
8 cloves garlic, smashed
1 ½ cups white vinegar
1 cup water
2 Tbs. kosher salt, divided in half
1 tsp. black pepper
2 tsp. turmeric
¼ cup avocado oil

TOOLS

• 2 large, heavy pots
• Hand blender
• Strainer
• Large metal ladle
• Glass jars

DIRECTIONS

1. In a large, heavy pot, heat oil and sauté peppers, onions, and garlic.
2. Cook until veggies are caramelized well; add 1 Tbs. salt and mix well.
3. Add water, vinegar, black pepper, and turmeric.
4. Cook over low to medium heat for about 45 minutes.
5. Let cool for about 10–15 minutes.
6. Blend directly in pot until sauce is smooth.**
7. Using another large heavy pot the same size as the first, take a small mesh strainer and hang onto second large pot.
8. Slowly pour a few cups of the sauce at a time into strainer and use a large, metal ladle to press; continue this process until liquid is through.
9. Discard pulp and chunks.***
10. Once strained, transfer to glass jars, deli containers, or holiday jars for gifts and/or storage.
11. Keep refrigerated.

Special Notes
Depending on how hot you like it, add 15 for most fire and 10 for least!
** Now the kinda messy, not-so-fun part.*
*** I usually keep a trash can nearby for pulp.*

QUICK FARMER PICKLES

Prep time: 1 hour
Servings: 6-8

This is a fun, quick recipe that can be used year round and is a great way to use up extra produce from the garden, or excess veggies in the fridge. This recipe originated when I was living in Chattanooga, Tennessee. It was used for a newspaper article about farmers markets, which are something I've always supported and tried to educate people who eat with me or work for me. This recipe has been tweaked a little since then. Please feel free to interchange the vinegars, vegetables, fruits, and spice varieties to go with whatever season it is.

INGREDIENTS

2 cups fresh cauliflower, cleaned and broken down into bite-size pieces
2 cups carrots, peeled and cut on the bias (diagonally)
2 red bell peppers, cleaned and cut in lengthwise strips
1 yellow onion, cleaned and julienned
½ cup fresh garlic, cleaned and smashed
½ cup fresh dill, roughly chopped
2 cups apple cider vinegar
1 cup water
1 ½ cup sugar
1 cup kosher salt
1 Tbs. peppercorns
1 Tbs. dill seed

TOOLS

• Peeler
• 2 large casserole dishes
• Medium, heavy saucepot
• Jars

DIRECTIONS

1. In a large casserole dish, lay vegetables out flat and reserve.
2. In a medium, heavy saucepot, bring vinegar, garlic, dill, salt, sugar, and spices to a soft boil.
3. Pour hot liquid directly over pickling vegetables.
4. Place a second casserole dish the same exact size over the pickling vegetables and press together tightly and carefully.
5. Let vegetables come to room temperature.
6. Transfer pickled vegetables to jars or deli cups and keep in fridge for 7-10 days before serving.

FOOD TUNES
"Electric Relaxation"
by A Tribe Called Quest

HOT DOG NEGRONI

Prep time: 5 minutes
Servings: 1

This recipe is not at all what you think it is! Hair of the (HOT) Dog Pub was a sister restaurant/pub to the Terminal BrewHouse in Chattanooga, Tennessee. It was the best industry spot in town and still one of my top spots for a drink and some good, honest pub eats. I also got to work there very briefly while opening Beast + Barrel with Matt and Ryan from the Terminal BrewHouse. I wanted to dedicate a recipe to HOT Dog Pub, and I hope this represents Matt and the pub well.

INGREDIENTS
1 ½ fluid oz. gin
½ fluid oz. dry vermouth
1 fluid oz. Campari®
½ fluid oz. simple syrup or agave
¼ orange, squeezed
Ice
Lemon twist

TOOLS
• Shaker
• Glass

FOOD TUNES
"It Was a Good Day"
by Ice Cube

DIRECTIONS
1. Place gin, vermouth, Campari, simple syrup, and orange juice into shaker with ice.
2. Mix well and pour into a glass (any size).
3. Garnish with a lemon twist.

SPOON'S SAUSAGE BALLS

Prep time: 10 minutes
Cook time: 20–25 minutes
Servings: 6–8

Spoon is, and will forever be, one of my besties. I met him through my wife when living in Chattanooga. We have a lot in common, like food, sports, and house music, but unfortunately, he's a Patriots fan. I still love him anyway. I got to spend a lot of time with him living in Chattanooga, working together and spending holidays together cooking and playing music. This is his sausage recipe, and it is a breakfast type of sausage but is great for a snack addition to Sunday Fundays!

INGREDIENTS
5 lbs. ground pork
½ cup apple cider vinegar
¼ cup + 1 Tbs. sugar
¼ cup + 1 Tbs. ground sage
¼ cup + 1 Tbs. dry oregano
1 Tbs. crushed red pepper
3 Tbs. kosher salt
2 tsp. black pepper

TOOLS
- Small mixing bowl
- Large mixing bowl
- Cooking spray
- Baking sheets

DIRECTIONS
1. Preheat oven to 350 degrees.
2. Mix apple cider vinegar, sugar, sage, oregano, red pepper, salt, and pepper in a small mixing bowl and reserve.
3. In a large mixing bowl, dump spice mixture over ground pork and mix well by hand.
4. Portion and roll into 2-oz. balls onto greased or lined baking sheets.
5. Bake for 20–25 minutes.
6. Let stand for 10 minutes and hope for an Eagles win today!

FOOD TUNES
"Affirmative Action"
by Nas

YOUR HOUSE-MADE TORTILLA CHIPS

Prep time: 20 minutes
Cook time: 48 minutes
Servings: 4-6

This is a fun, quick, homemade chip that will definitely impress your game guests and the kids will eat them too! I paired these with beer cheese dip, but these are great for nachos, huevos rancheros, or chips and salsa. After making, these will keep for about two days.

INGREDIENTS
24 white or yellow corn tortillas
1 cup avocado oil (any high smoke point oil will work)
Kosher salt

TOOLS
- Baking sheets
- Frying pan
- Paper towels
- Metal tongs or slotted spoon

DIRECTIONS
1. Preheat oven to 200 degrees.
2. Cut tortillas into fourths.
3. Dry tortillas in oven for 10 minutes on baking sheet.*
4. Heat oil until sizzling or 350 degrees in frying pan.**
5. Fry tortillas in small batches, not crowding the pan, and keep them moving around with metal tongs or a slotted spoon.
6. Fry for 2 minutes per batch until slightly browned.***
7. Season with salt while still warm.
8. Serve.

Special Notes
You will have to do this in batches. This will help with frying as you are pulling some of the moisture out.
**Have a large baking sheet layered with dry paper towels (to catch the oil) next to where you are frying.*
***Continue this process until all your chips are cooked. I typically take whatever oil is left over and try and recycle it when possible.*

FOOD TUNES
Any mix by the
magnificent DJ Jazzy Jeff

BEER CHEESE DIP

Prep time: 5 minutes
Cook time: 20 minutes
Servings: 4-6

All right! Everybody who's into entertaining for game day has a version of cheese dip. This is a hybrid I put together, combining beer and cheese. It doesn't get much better than this! Since I'm living back in Asheville these days, Highland Brewing's Gaelic® Ale would be my go-to beer. When in Chattanooga, it would be Terminal's Rock Out with Your Bock Out Maibock. Use something local and amber in color wherever you are.

INGREDIENTS

16 oz. White Kraft® Deluxe Style American
  Cheese (in block form), cubed
8 oz. smoked gouda cheese, grated
½ cup whole milk
¼ cup amber ale
2 tsp. cumin
Pinch of cayenne pepper
1 Tbs. unsalted butter

TOOLS

- Medium, heavy saucepot
- Whisk

DIRECTIONS

1. In a medium, heavy saucepot, place all ingredients and heat very slowly until all cheese is melted.
2. Stir occasionally until dip is a creamy consistency.
3. Before serving, whisk slightly to ensure no lumps.
4. Serve immediately with chips recipe from earlier.

DEHYDRATOR JERKY

Prep time: 4 hours
Cook time: 10 hour
Servings: 8-10

Once you realize how easy it is to make homemade jerky, it will become a regular for game day or holiday presents—I guarantee it. There is a small investment here, but it's well worth it. You can get a home dehydrator for around fifty dollars. You can use it to dry your own herbs, make fruit leather for the kids, and, of course, create any kind of jerky you want. I lay out a simple basic recipe below, but by all means use your favorite marinade recipe or one of my favorites—buffalo style. Yep, wing sauce jerky! I am dropping the mic and walking to the kitchen now!

INGREDIENTS
1 lb. flank steak, fat removed*
¼ cup tamari sauce
¼ cup Worcestershire sauce
1 tsp. black pepper
1 Tbs. Tabasco® sauce
4 cloves garlic, smashed
1 tsp. smoked paprika

TOOLS
• Dehydrator
• Gallon Ziploc™ bags
• Medium mixing bowl
• Strainer

DIRECTIONS
1. Remove fat from flank steak and cut lengthwise into strips 2-3 inches long and 1 inch thick.
2. Place meat in gallon Ziploc bag in the fridge and prepare marinade.
3. Mix remaining ingredients well in mixing bowl.
4. Pour marinade over steak into Ziploc bag.
5. Marinate 2-4 hours.
6. After marinating, dump everything into strainer and pat dry.**
7. Spread jerky cuts onto the layered shelving of dehydrator.
8. Cook at 145 degrees for 8-10 hours.
9. Check progress about 4 hours in, and adjust time and temperature if needed.
10. Store in clean Ziploc bags at room temperature until ready to eat.

Special Notes
I prefer flank steak because you can cut your jerky more uniformly, and it marinates well and fast!
**Do not skip the patting. Getting as much of the marinade off before transferring to dehydrator is crucial for cook time and final texture.*

SUNDAY FUNDAY BEERTAIL

Prep time: 5 minutes
Servings: 1

If you are unsure what Sunday Funday is, this is your chance to start life over and have some real enjoyment on Sunday afternoons. Honestly, it's just a reason to celebrate being with friends and family and an excuse to do some day drinking, but be festive about what you drink. This is a great beer cocktail to try out. This concept was one I discovered in Chicago but really got to play around with and come up with some great creative beverages at Terminal in Chattanooga.

INGREDIENTS
12 fluid oz. of your favorite lager or American pale ale
1 fluid oz. whiskey
2 oz. ginger beer
1 dash bitters
½ oz. fresh lime juice
Lime twist
Ice

TOOLS
- Shaker
- Pint glass

DIRECTIONS
1. Add whiskey, ginger beer, bitters, and lime juice into shaker with ice cubes and shake.
2. Strain into a pint glass and top with beer.
3. Garnish with a lime twist.

Philadelphia Bar & Restaurant

...ES AT $6 EACH

e and Smoked Gouda 7

SUGGESTED BEER PAIRING

5oz,   8oz,   full pour

...ons, wild ricecake,

MOO HOO:
CHOCOLATE MILK STOUT
$2, $3.5, $7

...a bed of country grits

HOPSECUTIONER: IPA
$1, $2, $5

...mento cheese

OAK AGED BIG HOPPY MONSTER:
IMPERIAL RED ALE
$2, $4.5, $8.5

...mushrooms,

MONK'S REVENGE:
IMPERIAL BELGIAN IPA
$2, $4.5, $8.5

...heese, fresh

WAKE N' BAKE:
COFFEE OATMEAL STOUT
$2, $4.5, $8.5

...PLATE:
...sonal fruit, Ale musta...
...airings for 6

...BEET SALAD:
...d almonds, balsamic

...IE CHOUX:
...e creamed corn 7

...ORNIA BURGER:
...bacon, avocado, goat ch...

...Y FLATBREAD:
...aised short rib, provolone, sa...
...Stout braised onions 10

..."...FUL BREAD" FLATBREAD:
...n Ale braised shrooms, roasted red pe...
...cheese, balsamic reduction 10

...ICHOKE FRITTERS:
...emon cream dip 8

...KOLCH MUSSELS:
...ano peppers, red pepper, Liscios crostini,
...P.B.C. Kenzinger. 10

...er or undercooked meats, poultry,
...increase your risk of food borne
...certain medical conditions

DESSERTS

...CHOCOLATE STOUT...
...ake, Ganache, Vanilla \...

FRIED OREOS:
Caramel dipping sauce

FEATURED LARGE BOT...

SIERRA NEVADA, HARVEST...
American IPA (6.7%)   14...
RARE NEBRASKA, FATHEAD...
Barleywine (11.3%) 33

The O'Jays, The Delfonics, Blue Magic ... the sound of Philadelphia. This is a sound I unfortunately didn't get into until later in life. Since then, however, I have fallen in love with this precious, moving style of music and have become a collector of many of these tunes on vinyl.

JERICHO MICHEL
EXECUTIVE CHEF
jericho.michel@bowlluckystrike.com

P 215.545.2471   C 773.612.1337   F 215.732.1074

LUCKY STRIKE
1336 CHESTNUT ST.
PHILADELPHIA, PA 19107

bowlluckystrike.com

...ER
...E FIELD   GAME NUMBER

1
1978

PHILADELPHIA
Pennsylvania

2013-2014(ISH)

In 2013, I left the South (but not for good, by any means). I loved my job and the guys in Chatt, but something was calling me home. I grew up in South Jersey just across the bridge, though I always claimed Philly as home. It's a great city that fascinates me each time I return, which is about once per year.

My first dive into Philly's culinary scene was at a small pub-style kitchen I took over in Old City. It was run by three guys who loved working together, but didn't really know much about running a kitchen. The TV show "It's Always Sunny in Philadelphia" came to life. The show is about a group of friends who run a pub in Philly (poorly) and get into all kinds of trouble together. And for the record, I loved all three of these guys, but pub kitchen life was not for me. I like getting up in the morning for work—not sleeping in till noon to work night shifts.

Anyway, I took over a borderline failing kitchen, and learned how to revamp a dull menu at a place previously managed by a line cook. It was a lot tougher than I expected, but I pushed forward and taught the staff good habits.

I also learned how to make a proper cheesesteak, which may secretly be the reason I went back home. When it comes to cheesesteaks, tourists always argue over two spots: Gino's and Pats. Honestly, I don't prefer either; Campo's in Old City is my favorite and that is where my wife and I go every time. I will be hated for this, but it's my truth, my cheesesteak, and my cookbook! Ha!

I had fun building a beer-heavy bar menu and got comfortable playing with mussel specials. My time there was short-lived, but I'll never forget cooking in Old City. It was a proud moment in my career as I was not the only one in my family to cook in this great city. My aunts and uncles all cooked or served in Philly as well.

I also did a stint at a corporate gig in Center City. It was a place kind of like Dave and Buster's, an entertainment venue with bowling, pool tables, and catered events. This was my first corporate job as a chef, and I was in love until I realized I had fifteen bosses! I quickly learned the science behind working numbers, and I was held to keeping food and labor costs to a low I never knew was possible. The job frequently had me working three stations at once, delivering food to tables, and prepping for events by myself. This was not my favorite time, but it did make me look at the big picture and realize the industry is always about numbers.

While I loved the time spent back home, I soon returned to the South to open a new restaurant with my Chattanooga guys.

Jericho Michel 73

FOOD TUNES
"Love Train"
by the O'Jays

CHEESESTEAKS, OF COURSE

Prep time: 15 Minutes
Servings: 4

Yes, the title is correct. Just cheesesteak—not Philly, Philly cheesesteak, or steak and cheese. I've lived in quite a few places and have heard all the incorrect ways to say "cheesesteak." Living in New Jersey and Philly for a good part of my life, this is a sandwich I'm proud to talk about and create for people who have never had an authentic one. I'm sure there's someone out there, maybe a lot of someones, who will say my version lacks something as well. I accept the feedback, but here is my best version of what I would consider a real cheesesteak. (And, by the way, if you're reading this and you're a fan of football—yes, I'm an Eagles fan. Go Birds!)

Caramelized Onions

INGREDIENTS
3 cups of yellow onions, thinly sliced
¼ cup oil
2 tsp. salt
1 tsp. black pepper

TOOLS
• Large, heavy sauté pan or large skillet

DIRECTIONS
1. Heat pan and add oil.
2. Once oil is sizzling, add your onions and cook over medium heat so onions can caramelize.
3. Add salt and pepper and continue to break onions down until they are sweet, lightly brown, and almost candied.
4. Scrape from pan and reserve in small bowl.

Special Notes
Do not clean your pan/skillet. You're going to cook the steak right on that pan, and the steak will pick up the flavors left from the onions.

Cheesesteaks

INGREDIENTS
2 lbs. rib eye, thinly sliced. (You may get a funny look from your butcher depending on where you live).
4 9-inch hoagie rolls (my favorites are Liscio's or Amoroso's)
12 slices Boar's Head® white American cheese or Cooper® Sharp White
2 tsp. salt
1 tsp. black pepper

TOOLS
• Pan or skillet
• 2 metal spatulas (or spatula and metal tongs)

DIRECTIONS
1. Get your pan/skillet nice and hot.
2. Add your rib eye and start breaking down with 2 metal spatulas or one spatula and a set of metal tongs.
3. Continue until meat is slightly brown, then add salt and pepper and your caramelized onions.
4. Continue to cook and break down for about 3-5 more minutes.
5. Place 3 slices of cheese in each hoagie roll.
6. Divide your meat and onions into 4 piles; You may have to do this twice depending on your pan.
7. Tent meat and cheese over bun, leaving some space around the edges, then toast open-faced. This will provide nice, crispy edges while keeping your hoagie soft and chewy on the inside. (It's a Philly thing.)

Jericho Michel 75

JC'S BUTTER BEANS

Prep time: 24 hours
Cook time: 1 hour
Servings: 6

Jon Carl, as I said previously, will always have a special place in my heart and in a lot of the meals I cook, both at home and for a living. He was one of the first chefs who made me realize beans and legumes have a place on simple to extravagant menus, and I hope this recipe does justice to beans.

INGREDIENTS

4 cups dry butter beans*
1 medium yellow onion, roughly chopped
3 cloves garlic, smashed
1 medium carrot, sliced lengthwise
½ cup fresh fennel with leaves
2 bay leaves
4 sprigs fresh thyme
1 ½ Tbs. kosher salt
2 tsp. black pepper
2 tsp. dry oregano
½ cup white wine
2 Tbs. unsalted butter
8 cups water or stock**

TOOLS

• Large cooking pot

DIRECTIONS

1. In large cooking pot with 8 cups of water or stock, simmer beans, onion, garlic, carrot, fennel, thyme, and bay leaves for 45 minutes.
2. Once slightly tender, add salt, pepper, oregano, white wine, and butter and cook for 10-15 minutes.
3. Finish with salt and remove from heat; keep stirring until cool enough to serve and eat.

Special Notes
*To soak or not to soak ... I definitely believe that soaking beans ahead of time helps with cooking time and overall tenderness, but if you forgot to do it the night before, no worries—there is hope! That being said, if you choose to soak, cover completely with water in the pot you are going to cook them in for 2-24 hours.
** Stock will add more flavor but is not necessary.*

FOOD TUNES
"Darlin' Darlin' Baby
(Sweet, Tender, Love)"
by the O'Jays

Jon Carl

I met JC when I started with the Hearty Boys. He was the chef at the guys' restaurant called HB. Jon Carl is someone who made an immediate impact on me, and his food and personality was—and still is—awe-inspiring. He always said what was on his mind and said it with passion. Oh yeah, he is from Philly too. Every time I had the chance, I would spend time with JC, whether it be eating at HB to dine on his incredible food or just catch up and vent about my day. HB was a Bring Your Own Bottle (BYOB) restaurant, so I always brought him a bottle of bubbles to try and get him to join me, if only for a single drink and a hello. It usually worked as long as I went in early on a Tuesday. It took me years to understand why I always appreciated his style and technique. He represents pure comfort when he presents his food, and you can taste his passion and honesty in each and every plate he puts out. I realized later in life, once I was truly honest about my dishes and relaxed while preparing them, that that's what he nailed years ago in my world, and it is a great feeling to actually know what you represent in this crazy culinary world. I will never forget the talks, drinks, and good times I spent with JC.

I still keep in touch with him now. He has since then owned and operated two restaurants in Chicago but has moved back to Philly, where he owns and operates two fantastic spots that truly represent him and his love of food. I try and stop by when I am in town. I still bring a bottle of bubbles to try and lure him to my table for a chat.

BROCCOLI RABE

Prep time: 5 minutes
Cook time: 10 minutes
Servings: 2–3

Rabe is one of my favorite vegetables and is a great side you can sauté, grill, or oven roast. It has a slightly bitter flavor like radicchio but not as intense. It's also a great addition to hot, Italian-style hoagies. This is a simple, quick sauté dish, and you can replace the rabe with any similar vegetable if you can't find rabe or just want to try something different with your sauté skills.

INGREDIENTS

2 large bunches of broccoli rabe, tough
  non-leafy stems removed
2 Tbs. olive oil
1 ½ tsp. salt
½ tsp. garlic powder
½ tsp. black pepper
½ lemon, juiced

TOOLS

• Large sauté pan

DIRECTIONS

1. In a large sauté pan, heat olive oil
    to sizzling.
2. Add rabe and keep pan moving
    until cooked.
3. Add lemon juice.
4. Finish with salt, pepper, and garlic powder.
5. Serve immediately.

FOOD TUNES
"Didn't I (Blow Your
Mind This Time)"
by The Delfonics

"CITYWIDE"

Prep time: 5 minutes
Servings: 1

If you ever lived in or spent a good amount of time in Philly, you know exactly where I'm going with this. At first I thought about trying to create my own recipe using Citywide ingredients, but then I decided to keep it true to Philly and just go with the original recipe. Gotta represent! This is a special that runs all through the city, and it's just a cheap beer and a shot for a good price. A Philly happy hour, if you will. My take is found below.

INGREDIENTS
1 can Yuengling® or Dock Street
  Bohemian Pilsner
1 shot bourbon or whiskey
1 pickle back*

TOOLS
• 2 shot glasses

DIRECTIONS
1. Drink beer.
2. Follow with bourbon shot.
3. Chase with pickle back.

Special Notes
* I like to add a pickle back (shot of pickle juice). It makes the booze go down easier.

FOOD TUNES
"I'll Be Around"
by The Spinners

FOOD TUNES
"Just Don't Want to
Be Lonely" by Blue Magic

OLD CITY STOUT PROJECT CHILI

Prep time: 20 minutes
Cook time: 1 hour
Servings: 6-8

I created the title of this recipe from a hop project idea I heard about in Chattanooga. It was from a brewer that used different types of local hops in his IPA at the time. I re-purposed the idea, living in Philly and working in Old City, by using different local stouts with a basic chili recipe. This recipe can be made with your favorite local brew. I would stick with amber or dark beers with low IBUs (International Bitter Units) or low hop levels. You could easily omit beef and add a plant-based protein if you are into veggie chili.

INGREDIENTS

5 lbs. ground chuck
2 tsp. salt
3 tsp. black pepper, divided
3 cups yellow onions, medium diced
2 cups green bell peppers, medium diced
2 cups red bell peppers, medium diced
1 large jalapeño, minced with seeds
2 28-oz. cans diced tomatoes, with juice
6 oz. canned tomato paste
12 fluid oz. local stout beer
3 cups black beans, liquid drained (page 16)
2 Tbs. kosher salt
1 ½ Tbs. ground cumin
1 ½ Tbs. ground coriander
¼ cup chili powder
1 Tbs. paprika
1 tsp. cayenne
1 lime, juiced
1 cup fresh cilantro

TOOLS

• Large stockpot
• Strainer

DIRECTIONS

1. In large stockpot, brown ground chuck for 8-10 minutes with 2 tsp. salt and 1 tsp. pepper.
2. Drain meat into strainer and reserve.*
3. Reheat stockpot until leftover fat is sizzling.
4. Add onions and green and red peppers and cook over medium, stirring occasionally for 10 minutes until tender.
5. Add beer, cumin, coriander, chili powder, paprika, cayenne, 2 tsp. pepper, and 1 Tbs. kosher salt and cook for 5 minutes.
6. Add canned tomatoes with juice, black beans, and ground beef and cook on low heat for 5-10 minutes.
7. Add tomato paste and simmer until chili is thick (the consistency of stew).
8. Right before serving, add remaining 1 Tbs. of kosher salt, lime juice, and cilantro.**

Special Notes

Don't clean your pot out. We are going to deglaze with veggies for the next step.
**My favorite add-ons for chili are chopped onions, shredded sharp cheddar, and pickled jalapeños, but you can add whatever you like to get to your chili happy place. Enjoy it with a stout!*

SPICY TUNA BURGER WITH LEMON-AIOLI SAUCE

Prep time: 20 minutes
Cook time: 6 minutes
Servings: 4–6*

This recipe was one of my near misses that became one of my favorite pub burgers. I came up with it while trying to get something fresh and (almost) healthy on a heavy burger-and-fry-type menu while working in Philly. You could easily turn these into sliders or make tuna balls if you are entertaining and want to try something to catch your guests' eyes.

INGREDIENTS

1 cup mayonnaise
¼ cup sour cream or yogurt
1 lemon, zested
½ lemon, juiced
1 tsp. salt
¼ tsp. black pepper
Pinch of cayenne
2 lbs. fresh sushi-grade tuna, cubed
1 ¼ oz. ginger
4 cloves fresh garlic, smashed and minced
1 ½ Tbs. tamari sauce
2 Tbs. scallions, julienned
¼ tsp. white pepper
1 Tbs. rice wine vinegar
1 ½ Tbs. jalapeños, diced small
1 Tbs. avocado oil

TOOLS

- Small mixing bowl
- Whisk
- Food processor
- Medium mixing bowl
- Large, heavy sauté pan

FOOD TUNES
"Only the Strong Survive"
by Jerry Butler

DIRECTIONS

1. Whisk mayonnaise, sour cream, lemon zest, lemon juice, salt, black pepper, and cayenne in small bowl; reserve and chill slightly.
2. In food processor, pulse down tuna until it has the consistency of ground chicken.
3. Transfer to medium mixing bowl and add ginger, garlic, tamari, scallions, white pepper, rice wine vinegar, and jalapeños.
4. Mix well by hand.
5. Form into patties by hand.
6. Chill for 30 minutes before searing.
7. Add 1 Tbs. avocado oil to large, heavy sauté pan and heat to sizzling.
8. Add burgers and cook on medium to high heat for 2–3 minutes per side.**
9. Top with Lemon Aioli and serve.***

Special Notes

This will make about six 6-oz. burgers or about five 8-oz. burgers.
**Cook longer if you prefer them cooked more than medium rare.*
***The best way to serve these is on a country white burger bun topped with lettuce, tomato, shaved red onion, and a dollop of the lemon aioli.*

KENDRICK'S KRAB DIP

Prep time: 10 minutes
Servings: 4

Kendrick is my daughter. She is one of my favorite people in the world and has taught me more in her first nine years than I could ever teach her. The name of this recipe is just because we were watching a lot of "Sponge Bob Square Pants" together when we lived in Philly. This a great, simple recipe to throw together for get-togethers or while watching the Flyers play. Hockey is the only sport she has taken interest in so far.

INGREDIENTS
8 oz. lump crab meat
½ red onion, minced
½ red bell pepper, minced
1 Tbs. fresh garlic, minced
8 oz. cream cheese, softened
½ lemon, juiced
2 Tbs. Dijon mustard
½ cup mayonnaise
1 cup sharp cheddar cheese, shredded
2 Tbs. Cajun spice blend
1 tsp. smoked paprika
2 tsp. kosher salt
1 tsp. fresh black pepper

TOOLS
• Large mixing bowl

DIRECTIONS
1. In large mixing bowl, add crab and break apart gently by hand.
2. Add cheeses, Dijon mustard, and mayonnaise and gently mix.
3. Add onions, peppers, garlic, lemon, Cajun spice blend, paprika, salt, and pepper and mix gently.
4. Chill for 30 minutes before serving.

Special Notes
This is great to serve with some good crackers and fresh grapes.

SUNSET AT PENN'S LANDING

Prep time: 5 minutes
Servings: 1

INGREDIENTS
2 fluid oz. Espolon Reposado® Tequila
½ fluid oz. Triple Sec
½ lime, juiced
½ fluid oz. pineapple juice
Pineapple chunk
3 sprigs of mint
Ice

TOOLS
• Shaker
• Highball glass

DIRECTIONS
1. Add all ingredients into shaker with ice.
2. Shake well and strain into highball glass over ice.
3. Garnish with fresh pineapple and a mint sprig.

FOOD TUNES
"TSOP (The Sound of Philadelphia)" by MFSB

FOOD TUNES: DISCO!

Try Donna Summer, KC and The Sunshine Band, and Sister Sledge for starters. As a DJ, I have been playing house music for years, but I eventually realized that all or most of the samples in the songs I loved came from old disco records. Once I caught on, I was hooked on the originals!

ASHVILLE
North Carolina

PART 3: 2014-PRESENT

Here I go again … back to the mountains—with my family this time! My wife is originally from Asheville, and several years back, we had some major stressors and troubling losses in our family. Between Opening Beast + Barrel with the guys from Terminal and losing a dear friend and then an uncle, I was emotionally worn out, to say the least. Heading to Asheville again seemed to make sense for both of us.

Asheville can be quite a healing place during tough times. Up until then, I hadn't really thought about what was next in my career, but I knew I needed to take a breather from full-on management and just cook for a while until I straightened out my head. (This obviously didn't last long if you guys have been following along with the book.)

Of all the places to hide in the corner and cook to pay the bills, I found myself, for the second time in my career, at The Laughing Seed Café. As you may remember, I had worked there briefly back in 2003. Joan and Joe are still the owners to this day, and Joan took me back—though she didn't fully understand why I wanted to be "just a cook" for a while.

That was when I met Parker. He and I were both line guys, and we bonded almost immediately, knowing we were both passionate and knowledgeable about what we do. When you've been in the business for this long, you just know, intuitively, which guys love to cook (and just happen to make money doing it), and which guys don't love to cook (but love the money they make for it).

It wasn't too much later that Parker and I joined forces and took over the kitchen at Laughing Seed. And when I say "took over," I mean we actually closed the place down, did a full remodel, and started from scratch. Joan loved the idea, and it was a mutual agreement; I was ready to get back into management, and she wanted to give Parker and me a shot to revamp the place. Rebuilding from the ground up was certainly a challenge, but one I was familiar with. After all, this was the third spot I had opened. So we got it together in order to reopen this Asheville milestone restaurant, and that's when things really started to get interesting.

Here, at the newly renovated Laughing Seed, Parker and I really got into hot sauce, pickling, and fermentation. He was the one who challenged me to make a great hot sauce—and I think I did okay! I pulled together a small hot sauce business and sold a little here and there locally. (You can read more about my hot-sauce journey in another chapter.)

CAMPFIRE FISH

Prep time: 10 minutes
Cook time: 18 minutes
Servings: 4

This is a great, surefire recipe that always impresses and is very easy to execute. I first tried a similar recipe like this while working in Chicago, but I have also had it on menus all around, and it works great while camping, if you are into that! This recipe is for home use, roasted in the oven, but works great on your backyard grill or smoker as well. We are going to use local North Carolina trout for this recipe, but you can always change up the type of fish you are using, and seafood works great as well. Whatever main ingredient used, keep the basic recipe the same and the weight of the fillet or seafood the same.

INGREDIENTS
4 6–8 oz. local trout fillets*
8 Tbs. unsalted butter
4 tsp. fresh dill, chopped and divided
4 cloves garlic, smashed, minced, and divided
4 lemons
2 large shallots, minced and divided
16 cherry or grape tomatoes, cut in half and divided
¼ cup white wine
4 tsp. kosher salt
2 tsp. black pepper
Dash of cayenne pepper

TOOLS
• 4 large pieces of foil big enough for fish to lay on and be wrapped in
• Large baking sheet

DIRECTIONS
1. Preheat oven to 375 degrees.
2. Lay out foil sheets and place one fillet on each, skin side down.
3. Season with salt, pepper, and cayenne.
4. Divide shallots, garlic, tomatoes, and dill evenly over each fillet.
5. Place 2 Tbs. of butter on each fillet.
6. Top each fillet with 1 Tbs. of white wine and the juice of half a lemon.
7. Wrap fillets individually, creating a pocket for the fish to cook in, making sure to cover completely.
8. Place fillet-filled foil packets on large baking sheet.
9. Roast for 12–15 minutes.
10. Unwrap the top of packets and roast for 3 minutes.
11. Remove from oven and top each fillet with lemon half.
12. Serve.**

Special Notes
This works best cleaned of all bones and with the skin on if available. Tilapia is a good substitute if trout is not available.
**You can serve this right out of the foil packet off the campfire or grill!*

FOOD TUNES
"Get Down Tonight" by
KC and The Sunshine Band

YEAST ROLLS

Prep time: 1 Hour 30 minutes
Cook time: 7 minutes
Servings: 40 mini rolls

I never got into baking bread until I moved back to Asheville for the third and (I think) final time. Baking bread always intimidated me, but an opportunity arose, and I spent a few weeks reading anything I could on the art and science of bread baking. I still have a lot to learn, but I have nailed some basics, and this is a simple recipe that anyone can make at home and add an artisanal touch. This recipe makes about 30-40 mini rolls. It seems like a lot, but throw what you are not going to use right away into the freezer for another meal. If you are going to go through the trouble of baking at home, make it worth your while. You can also change the size of these to 4 oz. and make burger buns instead.

INGREDIENTS
1 lb., 9 fluid oz. water, room temperature
5 fluid oz. olive oil
.6 oz. self-rising yeast
4 oz. sugar
3 lbs. 2oz. high gluten/bread flour
1 oz. kosher salt

TOOLS
- Kitchen scale
- 2 large mixing bowls
- Baking sheets
- Wax paper
- Cooking spray

DIRECTIONS
1. Preheat oven to 375 degrees.
2. In a large mixing bowl, add water and oil.
3. Sprinkle yeast and sugar into bowl.
4. Set aside for 10 minutes, and the yeast will bloom to a creamy consistency.
5. Slowly scoop flour in and mix well by hand, one hand adding the flour and one mixing it in.
6. Once flour is mixed in, add salt and turn onto a floured surface and knead well for 5 minutes.
7. Add dough ball into a clean, large, and greased bowl double the size of the current dough ball.
8. Spray top of dough and cover with plastic and let rise for 45 minutes to an hour, or until it has doubled in size.
9. Dump dough ball onto a floured surface and start cutting dough into 2 oz. balls formed by hand.
10. Transfer to baking sheets lined with wax paper and greased.
11. Bake 5 minutes.
12. Rotate and bake 2 minutes longer.
13. Let cool and serve immediately or freeze for later.

FOOD TUNES
"Last Dance"
by Donna Summer

T'S MIXED VEGGIES

Prep time: 5 minutes
Cook time: 8 minutes
Servings: 4

T in this recipe title refers to Teneka, a friend of mine and extended family from Chicago. I met her in the world of house music, a whole other part of my life we just touched the surface on in this book. Over the years, she has become one of my favorite DJs and family members. This particular recipe just needed a name, and she was on my list to get in this collection one way or another. This is a basic, quick sauté that uses broccoli and grape tomatoes, but remember the toolbox idea: you could easily change out the broccoli to cauliflower, summer squash, and so on.

INGREDIENTS
2 large bunches of broccoli, cut into 3" florets
1 pint grape or cherry tomatoes
¼ cup avocado oil
½ red onion, sliced thin
2 tsp. salt
1 tsp. black pepper
¼ cup white wine

TOOLS
• Large sauté pan

DIRECTIONS
1. In a large sauté pan, add oil and heat until sizzling.
2. Add broccoli and red onion.
3. Toss a couple of times, then add the tomatoes.
4. Cook for 3-5 minutes.
5. Add salt and pepper and cook for 3 minutes.
6. Once broccoli is slightly tender, or al dente, finish with white wine and cook until evaporated.
7. Serve immediately.

FOOD TUNES
"Got to Be Real"
by Cheryl Lynn

MY MICHEL MANHATTAN

Prep time: 5 minutes
Servings: 1

This is one recipe that's close to my heart. Some of my earliest memories as a kid were at my grandmom's house with her traditions and habits that I didn't appreciate until much later in life. As kids, we fought over the cherry from Grandmom's Manhattan. She liked hers pretty basic and to the point. I spiced my version up a bit but always think of her when I am making this or enjoying one with family.

INGREDIENTS
1 oz. whiskey*
2 oz. sweet vermouth
3 dashes bitters
1 Tbs. maraschino or Luxardo® cherry juice
1 maraschino or Luxardo cherry
Splash of orange liqueur
1 large whiskey ice cube**

TOOLS
• Rocks glass

DIRECTIONS
1. Mix all ingredients in a rocks glass over ice, stir, and top with a splash of orange liqueur.

Special Notes
* I prefer Crown Royal®!
** Regular ice cubes will work fine.

FOOD TUNES
"We Are Family"
by Sister Sledge

APPALACHIAN REMOULADE SAUCE

Prep time: 5 minutes
Cook time: 35 minutes
Servings: 8–10

This sauce can be a great finishing touch to a dish like the Campfire Fish (page 87) or T's Mixed Veggies (page 89) as well. You can show off and make a Cajun coleslaw using this base recipe or use it on po'boy-style sandwiches.

INGREDIENTS
1 ¼ cup mayonnaise
¼ cup Dijon or Creole mustard
2 tsp. smoked paprika
1 Tbs. hot sauce (page 75)
2 tsp. prepared horseradish
1 clove garlic, smashed and minced
1 Tbs. fresh thyme, chopped
1 tsp. dill pickle juice
1 Tbs. ketchup

TOOLS
- Small mixing bowl
- Whisk

DIRECTIONS
1. In a small mixing bowl, whisk all ingredients until incorporated well.
2. Chill for 30 minutes before serving.

FOOD TUNES
"Ring My Bell"
by Anita Ward

KEVIN LOVES MY MEAT
(OVEN-PULLED PORK)

Prep time: 20 minutes
Cook time: 6–7 hours
Servings: 10

have been making pulled pork in the oven for years. Yes, I know there is a pit master reading this and cursing me, but folks don't always have access to a smoker or know how to use one. This is as close as you can get to great barbecue by simply using the oven. Kevin is another old friend I consider extended family in my world of playing music. He is one of my biggest food fans, and yes, he does love my meat. You can definitely be the hit at any backyard barbecue with this dish.

INGREDIENTS

1 5-7-lb. pork shoulder/Boston butt, bone in
3 Tbs. smoked paprika
3 Tbs. brown sugar
3 Tbs. salt
2 Tbs. dry mustard
2 tsp. black pepper
1 Tbs. coriander
1 tsp. cayenne pepper
1 carrot, sliced lengthwise
1 onion, cleaned and cut into fourths
2-3 stalks celery, leaves attached
2 cups water
1 can local lager

TOOLS

• Small mixing bowl
• Roasting pan
• Plastic wrap
• Foil

DIRECTIONS

1. Preheat oven to 300 degrees.
2. Combine smoked paprika, brown sugar, salt, dry mustard, black pepper, coriander, and cayenne pepper and reserve.
3. Place carrots, onion, celery, water, and beer in a pan just big enough to fit the shoulder, with an extra 2–3 inches in the base for fat and liquid overflow.
4. Rub pork shoulder down with spice rub reserve and place on top of veggie and liquid mix.
5. Wrap over roasting pan first with plastic wrap and then foil to make sure pan is tightly sealed.
6. Cook 6–7 hours until meat is falling off the bone.
7. Let cool for 30 minutes before attempting to shred.

FOOD TUNES
"It's Raining Men"
by The Weather Girls

BEST CREAM CHEESE BROWNIES

Prep time: 15 minutes
Cook time: 22–25 minutes
Servings: 6

Aren't we all always looking for the best brownie recipe? I have been, and for years, I thought I had it. I was wrong! I took the best of my two favorites and … wait for it … this one is gluten- free! My wife is gluten intolerant, and I have unfortunately discovered that I am a little as well. I truly think we all are and just have to eat gluten in moderation. This is a truly guilt-free brownie, and I guarantee your friends or guests won't even know it's gluten-free.

Brownies
INGREDIENTS
2 oz. unsweetened chocolate
8 Tbs. unsalted butter
1 cup sugar
Pinch of salt
1 tsp. vanilla
1 cup Bob's Red Mill® Gluten Free 1 to 1
  Baking Flour
2 eggs

TOOLS
- Mixing bowls
- Baking pan (use your favorite brownie pan)
- Stand mixer
- Rubber spatula

DIRECTIONS
1. Preheat oven to 350 degrees.
2. Melt butter and chocolate together in microwave for about a minute.
3. Stir well and heat for 15 seconds longer.
4. In a large mixing bowl, cream sugar and eggs together.
5. Slowly drizzle in chocolate, butter, salt, and vanilla and continue to mix.
6. Add flour slowly and mix until everything is well incorporated.
7. Grease brownie pan.
8. Pour mixture in pan and spread evenly.
9. Bake 22–25 minutes until set.
10. Keep brownies in a cool part of your kitchen if you're eating right away or refrigerate them for the next day or a get-together later.

Icing
½ cup cream cheese, softened
½ cup butter, softened
½ cup vegetable shortening
1 tsp. vanilla
5 cups confectioners sugar

DIRECTIONS
While brownies are cooling make cream cheese frosting.

1. Add cream cheese, butter, shortening, and vanilla to mixer and mix on medium speed until well incorporated.
2. Slowly start adding sugar about ½ cup at a time.
3. Continue this until all 5 cups of sugar are added.
4. Chill for about 5–10 minutes before icing brownie.
5. Once brownies are room temperature, spread frosting with a rubber spatula.

SURSEE BEERTAIL

Prep time: 5 minutes
Servings: 1

During one of my many adventures over the years, I learned that "surcee" is a Carolinian term meaning "unexpected gift." This seems appropriate given that "Sursee" is also my good friend Alex's nickname. We do not have a shared past of cooking or food geek stuff in general, but we have been playing music together for well over twenty years. This is a beverage dedicated to the one-and-only Sursee.

INGREDIENTS
1 oz. bourbon
1 oz. coffee liqueur
2 dashes of cocoa bitters
6 oz. local stout or porter ale, chilled
1 orange twist

TOOLS
• Collins glass

DIRECTIONS
1. Pour bourbon, coffee liqueur, and bitters into a Collins glass.
2. Pour chilled stout or porter slowly on top.
3. Garnish with an orange twist.
4. Serve immediately.

FOOD TUNES
"Love Hangover"
by Diana Ross

WHAT IS KARL EATING NOW? CHEERWINE® BBQ SAUCE

Prep time: 15 minutes
Cook time: 30 minutes
Servings: 10

You guys should know Karl by now; he was our music pairing for Chicago. He has also been a fan and supporter of my food for many years now, and I tip my hat to him with this recipe. I've made a few different versions of this sauce. Root beer in Chicago, Cherry Coke® in Chattanooga, and now back in North Carolina, I figured Cheerwine would be suitable.

INGREDIENTS
1 cup yellow onion, roughly chopped
6 cups ketchup
1 cup yellow mustard
1 ½ cups Cheerwine soda
¼ cup apple cider vinegar
1 cup molasses
¼ cup honey
1 Tbs. salt
2 tsp. cayenne pepper
1 Tbs. smoked paprika

TOOLS
• Medium, heavy saucepot
• Hand blender

DIRECTIONS
1. Place all ingredients in a medium, heavy saucepot.
2. Simmer on low to medium heat for 30 minutes.
3. Once onions have cooked through, let cool for 15 minutes.
4. Blend until smooth and serve.

ECIPE

FOOD TUNES: JAZZ

This was the first style of music I really caught on to. It always makes me think about living in the great city of Philadelphia or hanging out with my family in New Jersey, and I can hear it playing in my head anytime I'm in a city just like the one I grew up in. My favorites have always been Miles Davis, John Coltrane, and Thelonious Monk.

CHOCOLATE SOUFFLE:

4 Egg Yolks

1/3

5 Ou

1 Tab

5 Egg

Ribbon

PASTRY

CAESAR DRESSING = 28 oz
3-EGG Yolkes - 1-CAN ANCHOVIES
3- CLOVES FRESH GARLIC - 1 oz
LEMON JUICE, 1 oz WHITE WINE.
2 oz WORCHESTER SHIRE SAUCE
3- HEAPING TSPs. POUPON MUSTARD.
2-CUPS OLIVE OIL 1½ CUPS CORN OIL
PUT GARLIC + ANCHOVIES IN BLEND
ER ON STIR, THEN ADD YOLKS, WINE
+LEMON JUICE. SLOWLY ADD OIL
IT WILL THICKEN, ADD FRESH

YIELD

SON, N.J.
776

MAPLE SHADE, N.J.
Michel

The Michel family's 60-year tradit

MY JOURNEY HOME

This chapter is dedicated to my family back in Jersey.

In it, I've included some stories and recipes from my childhood.

Grandpop's Turtle Soup

One of the few early childhood memories that I can recall surrounds my grandfather and his turtle soup.

Grandpop Joe was a chef at our family restaurant in Maple Shade, New Jersey, that was in our family for sixty-some-odd years. The restaurant was known as the German Kitchen before World War II; after that it was just called Michel's. My grandpa's brothers, Carl and Richard, also helped operate the family spot, and it was pretty well-known. They were true old-school culinarians. And, they had a popular seasonal dish they would prepare that was known all the way across the bridge into Philly: a snapping turtle soup they made once-per season.

My family's turtle soup brought in people from all over to scoop it up while it was still available. As far as I know, my grandfather and his brothers would actually go out and hunt the turtles themselves, fabricate them, and then prepare the soup. The one unfortunate memory I have of this is that Grandpop Joe would hang the turtles in the basement in Cinnaminson to bleed them out. The smell from that process is like nothing else I've ever encountered. I remember creeping down the basement steps to see what the awful smell was, but I never made it all the way down.

I know it's not exactly a great memory, but it connects me to my family and our food history. I have yet to make a turtle soup on my own (and you won't find that recipe in this book), but it's on my bucket list for sure.

Sunday Dinners at Grandmom Michel's

It was in Chicago, years later, that I learned how to entertain like a pro, but I will always remember our Sunday get-togethers at Grandmom's from when I was still a kid. They were always big productions, and everyone had something to contribute—whether it be shucking corn in the front yard, setting the table, pouring water, serving snacks, or making drinks. I was always excited about these dinners that included appetizers, a salad course (usually), an always-delicious main course, dessert, and after-dinner drinks. (The drinks were only for the adults, though us kids all got maraschino cherries from Grandmom's Manhattans on occasion.)

Those dinners were definitely my first peek at socializing with food and drink but also gave me a glimpse into fine dining. These days, I feel like it's so hard to get together with family the way we did back then: all at the same table, all talking and being merry. (Or at least pretending to be merry. Families don't always get along, as we all know.) I rarely get to see any of the Michel folks anymore—especially for large dinner gatherings—but I will always hold the moments I remember about them very close to my heart. Today, I still turn to memories of Michel family dinners for ideas when I throw grand dinner parties in my own home.

RATTEN

d Eye Roast

chopped
pped
celery chopped
e vinegar
er

ts in a deep dish. e eye roast for
emove from marinade and dry roast with a towel.
at 350 degrees. Turn occasionally for even
ace roast in pot and simmer
Remove the meat. Strain
water and 3 ounces of flour.

2 cups of cider vinegar
1 cup sugar
1/4 cup of Pickling Spices
salt & pepper to taste

Saute bacon and onions. Slowly add apples and
approximately 20 minutes. In another
sugar, salt and pepper. When
the vinegar, pickling spices,
into cabbage. Cook for about
with a cornstarch and cold wat

SPAETZEL

INGREDIENTS: 3 large eggs
                 5 1/2 ounces of   ounces all

nd beat well. Then a
um
o a
hin
er. Cook
ou can saute them

Jericho Michel 99

(The German Kitchen)

JOHNNY'S A-HOUSE WINGS

Prep time: 10 minutes
Cook time: 32 minutes
Servings: 2-3

The American House was a watering hole in Cinnaminson, New Jersey, that everyone in the family either spent time at—eating, drinking, or (a few of us) working as bartenders and/or servers at some point. It still stands today as Whistlers Inn, and when a few of us are close by, we find a reason to stop in for drinks and some of their (hopefully by now) world-famous wings. I remember my uncle Johnny making his version of these for family reunions or backyard get-togethers. He has since passed on, but hopefully he would be proud of my version of our family's A-House wings.

INGREDIENTS
12 chicken wings, bone-in, fat trimmed
Salt
Pepper
Cheerwine® BBQ Sauce (page 95) or
  Powers' Buffalo Sauce (page 102)

TOOLS
• Baking sheet
• Skillet

DIRECTIONS
1. Preheat oven to 375 degrees.
2. Season wings with salt and black pepper.
3. Lay wings flat on baking sheet.
4. Roast 30 minutes in oven.
5. Once cool to the touch, toss wings in sauce.
6. Grill for 1 minute on both sides in large skillet to caramelize.*

Special Notes
You can skip this finishing touch if you like, but it adds great flavor and texture!

FOOD TUNES
"My Baby Just Cares for Me" by Nina Simone

POWERS' BUFFALO SAUCE

Prep time: 5 minutes
Cook time: 10 minutes
Servings: 8-10

Now, making homemade buffalo sauce is quite easy, but you can always impress people coming over for the game or hanging out back for a get-together with this recipe. You can make the best impression here because you are going to make your hot sauce from scratch!

INGREDIENTS
2 cups Terminal Hot Sauce (page 63)
2 sticks butter, cold and cubed
1 tsp. cayenne pepper
½ tsp. black pepper
1 tsp. salt

TOOLS
- Medium, heavy sauce pot
- Whisk

DIRECTIONS
1. Slowly heat hot sauce in medium, heavy saucepot.
2. Once hot sauce is hot enough to melt butter, start adding butter cubes a few at a time, constantly whisking until all butter is added and melted.
3. Add salt, pepper, and cayenne.
4. Serve atop or with anything buffalo sauce is used for.

NANCY LEE'S OLD FASHIONED

Prep time: 5 minutes
Servings: 1

Never being much of a drinker, Grandpop Joe wanted something to toast the birth of his first grandchild, Deneen. Of course, owning a restaurant and having great bartenders provided Joe with the perfect means of finding that perfect drink. The bartender on duty that day was Nancy Lee, another chef in the family who was bartending at the time at Michel's. She had no problem coming up with the perfect cocktail for Joe who was, by no means, a serious-minded drinker and could not handle the taste of "rough spirits."

INGREDIENTS
1.5 fluid oz. bourbon whiskey
1 Tbs. simple syrup
1 tsp. maraschino cherry juice
2 dash bitters
1 slice fresh orange
1 maraschino cherry
Ice

TOOLS
- Muddler
- Shaker
- Rocks glass

DIRECTIONS
1. Muddle the orange and maraschino cherry in bottom of shaker.
2. Add bourbon, simple syrup, and cherry juice.
3. Shake with ice and strain into rocks glass with ice.

Special Notes
Story and recipe by Sue Michel. This became Joe's drink of choice when he wanted one.

BARNEGAT STEWED TOMATOES

Prep time: 10 minutes
Cook time: 30 minutes
Servings: 4-6

Barnegat, New Jersey, is a special place for me. I used to go there every summer for a week with no parents! I was with my aunt Sue and my cousin Deneen most summers. This was the one week I could let loose as a kid, and I remember going to the beach and the lighthouse and getting soft-serve ice cream cones. And, of course, the boardwalks! My daughter carries this tradition on and gets her week in at Barnegat every year since Sue has moved back up to New Jersey. This recipe is one that always makes me think of having fresh fish down on the shore as a kid. Jersey tomatoes are kind of a big deal, and this is my ode to them.

INGREDIENTS

10 large Jersey tomatoes*, cut into eighths
1 medium yellow onion, halved and sliced
3 Tbs. garlic, minced
2 Tbs. olive oil
½ lemon, juiced
2 sprigs fresh thyme
½ cup fresh parsley, chopped
½ cup white wine
1 Tbs. kosher salt
2 tsp. black pepper

TOOLS

• Large frying pan

DIRECTIONS

1. Saute onion and garlic in oil in large frying pan until soft.
2. Add tomatoes and thyme and cook uncovered until tender.
3. Season with salt, pepper, lemon juice, and parsley and add wine.
4. Cook covered for 20 minutes on medium heat.
5. Serve.**

Special Notes
Any local and in-season tomato will work, but I am biased!
** This acts as a great side or as a topping for freshly grilled fish.

FOOD TUNES
"Ruby My Dear"
by Max Roach Quartet

SAM'S GET-TOGETHER (CRAB CAKE)

Prep time: 2 hours 15 minutes
Cook time: 12–14 minutes
Servings: 4

I have a small group of friends who gather irregularly, say once-a-month, for dinner. This recipe was pieced together from conversations and meals shared on large porches and candlelit dining rooms. I haven't had a better crab cake anywhere.

INGREDIENTS

1 large egg
¼ cup mayonnaise
¼ cup parsley, chopped
½ teaspoon cayenne (optional for the timid)
2 tsp. Dijon mustard
2 tsp. Worcestershire sauce
1 ½ tsp. Old Bay® seasoning
2 tsp. lemon juice
1 lemon
¼ tsp. salt
1 lb. fresh lump crab
14 saltine crackers, crushed with rolling pin
2 Tbs. butter, melted

TOOLS

- Large bowl
- Rubber spatula
- Rolling pin
- Plastic wrap or foil
- Silicone baking sheets*
- ¼ cup measuring cup

DIRECTIONS

1. Mix together egg, mayonnaise, Dijon mustard, Worcestershire sauce, Old Bay seasoning, lemon juice, and salt in large bowl.
2. Add crab meat and cracker crumbs.**
3. Use rubber spatula to gently fold everything together.***
4. Cover mixing bowl tightly with plastic wrap or foil.
5. Refrigerate for 30 minutes or longer.****
6. Preheat oven to 450 degrees.
7. Use a ¼ cup measuring cup to make 12 mounds on greased silicone sheet.*****
8. Drizzle with melted butter.
9. Bake 12–14 minutes.
10. Squeeze lemon juice over crab cakes.
11. Sprinkle with chopped parsley.
12. Serve.

Special Notes

I use silicone baking sheets, lightly oiled. If you don't have those, just use a high quality, high smoke point oil like avocado or peanut on your rimmed baking sheet.
**Pay attention here!*
***Your mission is to not break apart those lumps of crab.*
****Don't skip this step. An hour or two is better. Overnight is fine if you like not being rushed the day of the dinner.*
*****Don't flatten the cakes! They will hold together and the heat will bind them. Use your hands to gently make sure no lumps are sticking out far enough to fall out.*

Recipe by Sam Wolfe.

FOOD TUNES
"A Love Supreme"
by John Coltrane

JEWISH APPLE CAKE

Prep time: 20 minutes
Cook time: 1 hour and 5 minutes
Servings: 8

This is one of my all-time favorite desserts to make. My mother and grandmother used to make this cake all the time when I was a kid. This is a recipe that I tried in my early baking days as a young chef and tried countless times to mirror what they would make when I was a child. After years of almost getting it right, I finally put one together that I am proud to share.

INGREDIENTS
1 ½ large Gala or Honeycrisp apples,
  seeded and chopped small
Pinch of cinnamon
Pinch of ginger
Pinch of nutmeg
3 cups all purpose flour or 3 ½ cups
  Bob's Red Mill® Gluten Free 1 to 1 Baking Flour
½ tsp. salt
2 tsp. cinnamon
2 ½ tsp. baking powder
2 cups sugar
1 cup oil
2 Tbs. vanilla
4 eggs
¼ cup apple cider
Fresh whipped cream
Vanilla ice cream

TOOLS
• Medium mixing bowl
• Large mixing bowl
• Bundt pan
• Pastry brush

FOOD TUNES
"Feeling Good"
by Nina Simone

DIRECTIONS
1. Preheat oven to 350 degrees.
2. Chop apples and toss with a pinch each of cinnamon, ginger, nutmeg, and sugar and reserve in medium mixing bowl.
3. Cream butter and eggs in large mixing bowl.
4. Mix in oil, cinnamon, sugar, salt, and vanilla.
5. Slowly add in flour and baking powder and mix.
6. Grease Bundt pan right before adding batter in layers.
7. Add half the batter into pan, then add half the apples and spice mixture.
8. Top with second half of batter and finish with remaining apples and spices.
9. Bake for 1 hour and 5 minutes.
10. Cool cake.
11. Brush cooled cake with apple cider on the base, then flip and brush the top.
12. Serve slightly warm with fresh whipped cream or vanilla ice cream.

FOOD TUNES
"A Night in Tunisia"
by Dizzy Gillespie

BEER-CAN CHICKEN

Prep time: 20 minutes
Cook time: 2 hours
Servings: 4-6

M y childhood memories of backyard get-togethers begin with the Powers side of my family. I'll always remember Grandmom and Grandpop's place in Burlington Township, New Jersey, where I lived for a short while, and my uncle Larry's place in Medford, New Jersey. There were always a few motorcycles out front and sometimes a lot of them. I always brought a friend to these events, and I remember how everyone would let their guard down and just shoot the breeze with a few beers and good, simple burgers, dogs, and potato salad. I put this recipe together because it doesn't get any more rustic and backyard than beer-can chicken.

INGREDIENTS
1 4-5 lbs. whole chicken
3 Tbs. BBQ rub*
12 fluid oz. can beer or local pilsner

TOOLS
• Grill**
• Paper towel
• Drip pan
• Wood chips
• Smoker box
• Church key can opener
• Tongs
• Cutting board or platter
• Metal spatula

DIRECTIONS
1. Remove and discard fat from inside cavity of chicken, rinse inside and out, and pat chicken dry with paper towel.
2. Rub 1 Tbs. of seasoning inside chicken.
3. Rub 1 Tbs. of seasoning on outside of chicken.
4. Set up the grill for indirect grilling and place a drip pan in the center. ***
5. Pop tab on beer can and use church key can opener to poke 6 or 7 holes in the top of the can.
6. Pour out or drink the top inch of beer.
7. Spoon remaining dry rub through the holes in can and into beer.
8. Hold chicken upright, with the opening of the body cavity down; insert beer can into the cavity.****
9. Oil the grill grate.
10. Stand chicken up in center of hot grate and over the drip pan by spreading out the legs to form tripod to support it.
11. Cover grill with lid and cook chicken until fall-off-the-bone tender, approximately two hours.*****
12. Using tongs, lift the bird to a cutting board or platter, holding the metal spatula underneath the beer can for support.******
13. Let stand 5 minutes before carving the meat off upright carcass.
14. Serve.
15. Dispose of beer can and carcass.

Special Notes
Recipe for BBQ rub can be found on page 93 or you can use 3 Tbs. of the pastrami rub on page 61.
** *Below are a few different tips and steps depending on what type of grill you are using.*
*** *If using a charcoal grill, preheat it to medium. If using a gas grill, place wood chips in the smoker box and preheat the grill on high; then, when smoke appears, lower the heat to medium.*
**** *If using charcoal, toss half the wood chips on the coals.*
***** *If using charcoal, add 10-12 fresh coals per side and remaining wood chips after 1 hour.*
****** *Have the board or platter right next to the bird to make the move shorter. Be careful not to spill hot beer on yourself!*

JERSEY CREAMED CORN

Prep time: 10 minutes
Cook time: 15 minutes
Servings: 6-8

I will tell you a secret: I hated creamed corn growing up, but when I was in Chattanooga, Tennessee, my boss at the time wanted a side dish that represented my palate and past. So I developed this, and have loved this real homemade creamed corn recipe ever since. This is one I hope my family and yours can add to your picnic menus or maybe even Thanksgiving.

INGREDIENTS

1 ½ qt. fresh corn, kernels only
½ large red onion, diced
1 red bell pepper, diced
2 cloves garlic, smashed and minced
¼ lb. unsalted butter
1 cup heavy cream
2 tsp. kosher salt
1 tsp. black pepper
1 tsp. smoked paprika

TOOLS

- Large, heavy saucepan
- Mixing bowl
- Hand blender

DIRECTIONS

1. Melt butter in large, heavy saucepan.
2. Add red onion, garlic, and red bell pepper and sauté until tender.
3. Add corn and simmer for 5 minutes.
4. Turn off heat and take ⅓ of corn and veggie mix out and place into a mixing bowl.
5. Blend with a hand blender, keeping some texture.
6. Add mixture back to pan.
7. Bring up to a simmer.
8. Add cream, salt, and pepper and simmer until slightly thick.
9. Serve.

Special Notes

A great addition to this recipe is to go Cajun-style: just add some Cajun seasoning and a few dashes of Tabasco® sauce to spice it up!

FOOD TUNES
"Watermelon Man"
by Herbie Hancock

ROY'S PICKLED SHRIMP

Prep time: 20 minutes
Cook time: 5 minutes
Servings: 4-6

This is my go-to recipe when I need to take an appetizer somewhere. My dad loved this shrimp!

INGREDIENTS

2-2 ½ lbs. shrimp, peeled and deveined
1 large red onion, sliced thin
4 bay leaves
1 cup vegetable oil*
¾ cup white vinegar
¼ cup red wine vinegar
2 Tbs. fresh lemon juice
1 Tbs. Worcestershire sauce
3 Tbs. capers
2 ½ tsp. celery seed
1 ½ tsp. salt
2 tsp. hot sauce

TOOLS

- Frying pan
- 2 glass mixing bowls
- Whisk
- Plastic wrap

DIRECTIONS

1. Lightly season the shrimp and grill or sauté until cooked through.
2. Place in glass serving bowl or baking dish and top with onion slices and bay leaves.
3. Whisk together oil, vinegars, and lemon juice until emulsified in separate bowl.
4. Stir in remaining ingredients and pour over shrimp mixture.
5. Cover and chill 2-8 hours.
6. Serve.

Special Notes
I use avocado oil!

Recipe by Beverly Wolfe.

JERSEY BACKYARD GARDEN SALAD

Prep time: 10 minutes
Servings: 4-6

Even though most people don't think of New Jersey as the Garden State, it is very well-known for its seasonal produce—tomatoes being the most famous one, at least where I grew up just outside of Philly. I remember small produce stands with only one sign that said "Jersey Tomatoes," and that was enough to make you pull over on the way to a get-together in the summertime. This is a quick, simple recipe using fresh ingredients that will always impress, and the kids might eat it as well.

INGREDIENTS

4 cups assorted seasonal small tomatoes,
  cut into bite-sized pieces
2 large cucumbers, seeded and diced medium
½ cup red onion, sliced thin
1 bunch parsley, stems removed and
  roughly chopped
¼ cup olive oil
⅛ cup champagne vinegar
1 Tbs. salt
2 tsp. black pepper

TOOLS

• Large bowl

DIRECTIONS

1. Toss all ingredients into large bowl.
2. Chill 30 minutes before serving.

IRISH LEMONADE

Prep time: 5 minutes
Servings: 1

This seemed like a perfect symbolic fit for the Powers' drink to best represent backyard gatherings. I have had my fair share of Jameson® with my uncles, dad, and brother, so I came up with this. If whiskey is too tough for you, swap it out for vodka or gin.

INGREDIENTS
2 fluid oz. Jameson whiskey
1 fluid oz. simple syrup
1 fluid oz. fresh lemon juice
½ fluid oz. sweet vermouth
1 dash bitters
Soda water
Lemon twist
Ice

TOOLS
- Shaker
- Collins glass

DIRECTIONS
1. Add all ingredients in martini shaker with ice.
2. Shake well.
3. Strain into a Collins glass with ice.
4. Top with soda water.
5. Garnish with lemon twist and serve.

FOOD TUNES
"Bitches Brew"
by Miles Davis

INDEX